441796

D1588829

THE ARCHITECTURE OF JACQUES FERRIER

WITHDRAWN FROM STOCK

THE ARCHITECTURE OF JACQUES FERRIER
Alexander Tzonis and Kenneth Powell

Thames & Hudson

Contents

I first heard Jacques Ferrier's name in 1993 from Étienne de Cointet, director of the school of architecture in Saint-Étienne and a friend and research colleague since the 1970s. He had suggested working together on a project to investigate design as a collaborative process in architectural practices, and one of the case studies was the young firm of Jacques Ferrier and François Gruson. Independently of the project's goals, I was struck from the beginning by the freshness of Ferrier's design-thinking and the architectural quality of his buildings, p. 31 in particular the Sagep Water Treatment Plant in Joinville-le-Pont, which he was working on at the time and was the subject of our investigation.

Ferrier's approach to architecture was also expressed in his occasional 'underground' journal, Dépliant, which contained essays from the 1950s by critics (Reyner Banham) and architects (Jaap Bakema). His ideas diverged from the dominant trend of the period (Postmodernism) and his early projects showed the promise of something altogether newer and more interesting. Postmodernism had emerged in the 1970s as a reaction against a lack of quality and humanity in the architecture that sprang from the ruins of the Second World War, and promised to overcome the negative effects of the unprecedented economic development that had led to millions of new buildings, changing cities beyond recognition. The record figures of GDP growth did not take into account the resulting environmental and human cost, and Postmodernism did not deliver what it promised. Most of its projects were only stylistically, rather than substantially, different from the mainstream architecture its adherents were meant to oppose and replace.

In most cases, the pseudo-historicist rhetoric adopted by the postmodernists failed in their aim to create civilized, healthy, lasting environments that were capable of facilitating happiness. No such rhetoric is present in Ferrier's scheme for the Sagep waterworks. The structure was highly technical, but not overly so. It was elementary and serene, but not severely minimalist. Many architects who shared the same dissatisfaction with the lofty, technophobic ambitions of postmodern architecture reacted by refocusing on technology to the exclusion of most of the other qualities that characterized a building termed as 'minimalist', a label borrowed from the dominant art movement of the period. Inspired by Mies van der Rohe's idea that 'less is more', architectural minimalists produced reductive buildings driven by stylistic concerns, without regard for even the most basic functional needs. (Mies famously removed the screens from Farnsworth House, in Plano, Illinois, which was built on wet land, thus condemning the client to be devoured by mosquitoes.)[1]

Ferrier's approach is different. We may call it 'essentialist' in the sense that its strictness and simplicity are the results of a commitment to the essentials of reality and not to an abstract ideal of making things minimal by reduction. As is evident in his scheme for the Sagep Water Treatment Plant and in his later designs, Ferrier rejects formalist one-dimensional ideas, respecting, rather than reducing, the human needs and aspirations associated with his commissions. The concrete blocks of the Sagep waterworks were put together with thoughtfulness and precision, and do not protrude or thrust into the space of people approaching the building. Despite their nakedness, the machine-made surfaces are not aggressive: they suggest respect for each other, rather than a narcissistic distance. They are there because they serve a purpose.

In all of his designs, Ferrier's attitude towards technology is unlike that of Mies or the minimalists. It comes close to the methods of Jean Prouvé, Max Bill and Charles and Ray Eames, but is also within the French architectural tradition that developed outside the École des Beaux-Arts. He never allows the product of technology to become an object of desire, whereas the minimalists were busy fabricating elegant, precious-looking, mostly non-functional artefacts.[2] Ferrier, like Prouvé, Bill and the Eameses, is driven by a project's programme, and how it might be served by the industrial and technological means at his disposal. For Ferrier, industrial products are 'givens', within which a problem has to be solved: they are 'off the shelf'; 'tools' for use; if possible, 'ready-made'. In this respect, his views about materials and technology recall Otto Neurath's idea of how scientific discovery works: not through minimalist abstractions, but through real, available material. Imagine sailors who try to reconstruct a leaking boat while at sea, Neurath wrote. To do so, they must reuse the timber from the old structure as they cannot start from scratch. Whenever an old beam is removed, another must replace it. Eventually, the entire boat is rebuilt.[3]

Ferrier's attitude towards design and technology also recalls the ideas of René Descartes, a similarity I have noted in the past.[4] Of course, using the term 'Cartesian' might be initially misleading, like the use of orthogonal coordinates and analysis. But by calling Ferrier a 'new Cartesian', I was referring to Descartes' 'Objections', published in his Meditations on First Philosophy (1641), in which the philosopher defends his preference for planned buildings by saying that they are more beautiful than old structures, which have merely been improved, and for cities

8

that are laid out on a grid over those that began as villages and evolved slowly from an irregular and haphazard mass of inherited ideas. Yet Descartes came to a surprising conclusion: one cannot rebuild a house that one lives in by pulling it down and starting over, altering and overturning everything.

Thus, as a 'new Cartesian', Ferrier 'recruits' his construction materials from an existing stockpile. He explores and exploits their properties opportunistically and creatively (as Charles and Ray Eames did with their house in Pacific Palisades, California, in 1949, part of the Case Study House programme set up by John Entenza). In this way, Ferrier is a 'techno-recruiter', reacting against impulsive novelty and addictive consumption. His design strategy satisfies the goals established by the modern sustainability movement. The Sagep Water Treatment Plant is not an autonomous object, set apart from its surroundings. And, in fact, even without emphasized edges and prominent profiles, owing to the rigorous geometry of their schemes, all of Ferrier's projects stand out — not in a grand and imposing manner, as with palaces or temples, but more modestly, like the ancient stoas whose configuration is part of a larger building network (real or implied). The Sagep project is calm but not dull. One is particularly seduced by the sensitivity and precision of the small-scale details, the surface joints of the blocks and the choice of industrial blue for the building's envelope.

The challenge of achieving technological quality in the building envelope as it defines the relationship between interior and exterior space has been a preoccupation of Ferrier's in all of his projects. This was a relatively new idea, because as science and economics have had an ever-more leading role in architectural thinking since the eighteenth century, it was construction — true, natural, essential — that was the driving force in design. The idea of cladding as an equally significant determinant of an architectural scheme emerged in the nineteenth century, with Gottfried Semper as an early advocate.[5] In his campaign for an 'essentialist modern architecture', Ferrier, along with many architects of his generation, rethought the potential of a building's skin beyond the fashion of the post-Miesian curtain walls, which proved, in most cases, to be functional failures. He used new materials that were highly resistant to ageing and weather conditions, promising to make real the architectural theorist Carlo Lodoli's vision of an architecture of eternal youth.

Ferrier moved away from the cliché of the curtain wall and experimented with a layered-envelope design approach. This permitted better environmental control and temperate transition from inside to outside, as well as generating the possibility of adding an extra usable space, a zone between the skin layers, which could be used for informal social interaction. Another unique aspect of Ferrier's work is his preoccupation with the plan as the generator of an architectural solution, rather than the façade or profile of a building. This can be seen in his reaction to whimsical postmodern schemes. Like many other aspects of his attitude towards design, however, the idea has its roots in the rationalist French thinking of the seventeenth and eighteenth centuries. Motivated by the need to accommodate movement in response to social pressures and a new way of life, the seventeenth-century French architect Augustin-Charles d'Aviler, together with other contemporaries, developed the concept of distribution, published in his popular Dictionnaire.[6]

'Distribution' refers to a design principle that organizes space according to use, unlike composition, which is concerned with the formal spatial organization of a building's elements. By the end of the eighteenth century, it assumed a greater importance with the introduction of a new design component, the corridor, which split the plans of buildings functionally, offering a degree of privacy to shield socializing residents from the noise and activity of the servants, while accommodating efficient and effective service. In the nineteenth century, following institutional and social change, the theoretician, teacher and architect Jean-Nicolas-Louis Durand systematized the idea of managing the space and function of new institutional buildings.[7]

But by the beginning of the twentieth century, the room-and-corridor principle of distribution was seen as antiquated, regimenting and fragmenting space, which led to the idea of a 'universal space' that would offer the highest possible degree of freedom of location and circulation, or so it was claimed. But this radical new solution also proved disappointing. Ever since the 1960s, many architects, including Shadrach Woods and Louis Kahn, have tried to explore new ideas, but these explorations remained mostly unfinished owing to the postmodern indifference to plans and functional innovations. From his very early work, focusing on the development of the plan of a building, Ferrier insisted on revising the idea of universal space. He searched for an organization of the plan that would differentiate functions between known and unknown, simple and difficult, certain and uncertain, well defined and unexplored, in order to enable old and new uses to evolve more freely.

Once again, Ferrier's idea of an architectural plan for our times with its system of controls and freedoms is reminiscent of Descartes's proposal for a way of thinking. Descartes wrote during a time of great upheaval, but it was also one of exploration and invention. In Rules for the Direction of the Mind (1628), he attempted to establish the necessary conditions required to enhance creativity, despite the uncertainty and hostile conditions of the age. Using an architectural metaphor, he argued for a strategy of the sustainable evolution of ideas. In many respects, the times in which he lived have strong similarities to ours. Reversing the analogy from abstract thinking to the concreteness of architecture, one could say that Ferrier's idea of the plan offers a direction for essential architectural conditions to enable human interaction, community and creativity, despite the adverse circumstances of modern life.

It was in Shanghai, says Ferrier, that the idea of the ville sensuelle was born. At about the same time, coinciding with the start of his collaboration with Pauline Marchetti, the city and the quality of the sensual environment became central in his thinking. The urban question was always present in Ferrier's approach to the design of a project, a view that is not typical of practising architects, especially in France and the US, where building design evolved under the shadow of Beaux-Arts trained architects, who looked at buildings as autonomous objects and the city as a collection of those objects. But in France there was another tradition that looked at buildings as tangible physical artefacts, constructed as part of a tissue, rather than as autonomous abstract formal compositions or as objects that stood apart from the rest of the world.

Soon after Ferrier's sensual-environmental awakening, there was the discovery of another region, the Mediterranean – or rather, rediscovery: we have already seen the special responsiveness with which Ferrier approached projects in the south of France. As with Shanghai, his fascination with the Mediterranean was its peculiar 'agreeable disorder', a description of nature used during the Picturesque movement in eighteenth-century England, compared to the regimented classical academic architecture of the continent. For Ferrier, this agreeable disorder was characteristic of the built tissue of these cities and their way of life, sensually luxuriant, as well as socially rich. 'Disorder' in this sense had both a psychological and political meaning.

After this experience, Ferrier began to write and research, adding the Californian coast to Shanghai and the Mediterranean. His writings ranged from sharp, empirical observations of how people live their lives, interacting positively, functionally and sensually with their human and natural environment, to suggestions about learning from and how to construct in these environments. Above all, Shanghai, the Mediterranean and the Californian coastline were positive utopian paradigms for a 'better city, better life', ecologically, sensually and socially, to use the slogan of the 2010 Shanghai Expo, for which Ferrier designed the French national pavilion H.

p. 179

p. 41

But in a non-utopian way, Ferrier became involved with a genuinely pragmatic urban-planning programme at about the same time for a series of metro stations for the Société du Grand Paris. It was to a great extent a technical problem that Ferrier as an engineer could command. But for his clients, and for Ferrier himself, it was a project that also asked for cultural quality, as well as environmental. Infrastructure, he felt, was as vital as buildings for modern happy life, and as culturally and sensually significant as a museum. The search for a sensual environment has a long history in Western culture, from Abbot Suger's synthesis of sensuality and piety at the cathedral of Saint-Denis, the fifteenth-century Hypnerotomachia Poliphili and the philosophical writings of Anthony, 3rd Earl of Shaftesbury to Jean-Jacques Rousseau's 'therapeutic' water geometry on an island in the middle of Lake Bienne and the 'artefacted boudoirs' of Nicolas Le Camus de Mézières.

In his critical lectures, published in The Crown of Wild Olive, John Ruskin warned about the coming environmental, social and sensual catastrophe. At the time, few people paid attention.[8] During the twentieth century, the issue of the sensual city continued to decline, especially after the Second World War, as discussed in the writings of Steen Eiler Rasmussen.[9] But soon these worries waned as explosive urbanization and 'starchitecture' took over, destroying environmental pleasures and increasing the gap between the few who still appreciate the joys of the senses, occasionally artificially supplied, and those almost totally deprived of them.

The recent shift in Ferrier's focus from the design of individual buildings, which he has done so successfully and creatively, to the city and the environment at large perhaps suggests that the accumulation of single buildings, even if they are 'star-buildings', is not enough to ensure lasting happiness.

1. Peter Blake, *Mies van der Rohe: Architecture and Structure* (Baltimore, 1964), pp. 85–9.
2. Stanislaus von Moos, *Minimal Tradition: Max Bill Today* (Zurich, 1996).
3. Otto Neurath, 'Foundations of the Social Sciences', in Otto Neurath, Rudolf Carnap and Charles Morris, *International Encyclopedia of Unified Science*, vol. 2, no. 1 (Chicago, 1944).
4. Alexander Tzonis and Liane Lefaivre, 'Innovation Cartésienne', in *Jacques Ferrier, Architecte* (Paris, 2000), pp. 30–43; Tzonis, 'Jacques Ferrier: A Techno-Recruiter Among the New Cartesians', in *Jacques Ferrier, Useful–Utiles* (Basel, 2004).
5. Tzonis and Lefaivre, 'Skin Rigorism: A New International Non-style', in *Casabella* 60:630–1 (1996):128–36.
6. Augustin-Charles d'Aviler, 'Distribution', in *Dictionnaire d'architecture civile et hydraulique et des arts qui en dépendent* (Paris, 1755).
7. Jean-Nicolas-Louis Durand, *Précis des leçons d'architecture données à l'École Polytechnique* (Paris, 1802–5).
8. John Ruskin, *The Crown of Wild Olive* (London, 1873).
9. Steen Eiler Rasmussen, *London: The Unique City* (London, 1937); Rasmussen, *Experiencing Architecture* (Cambridge, Massachusetts, 1962).

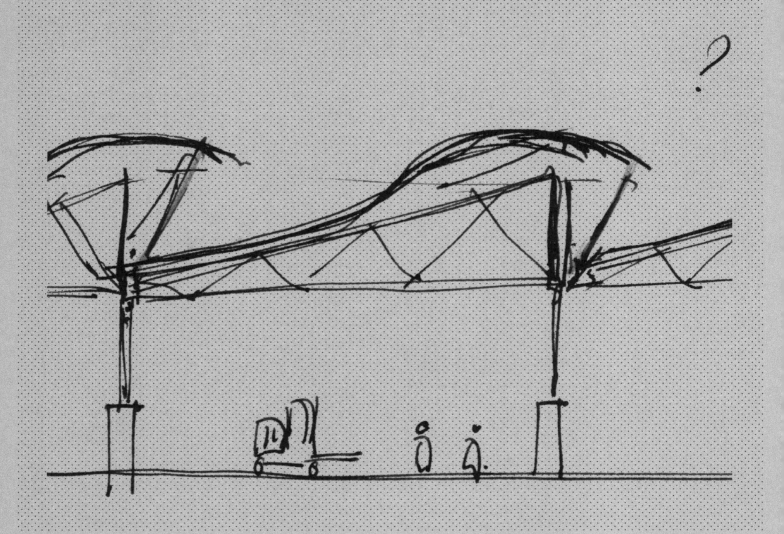

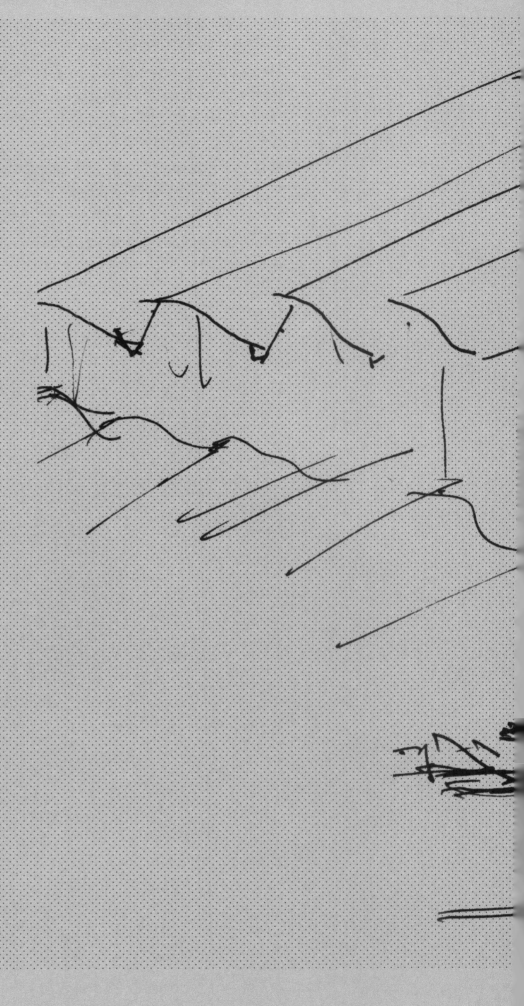

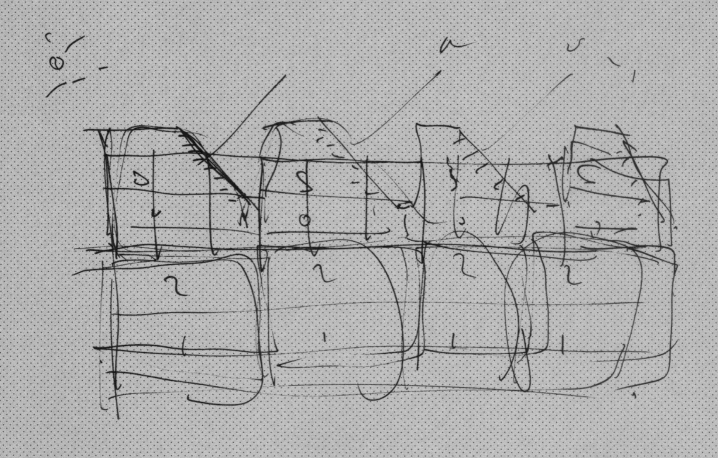

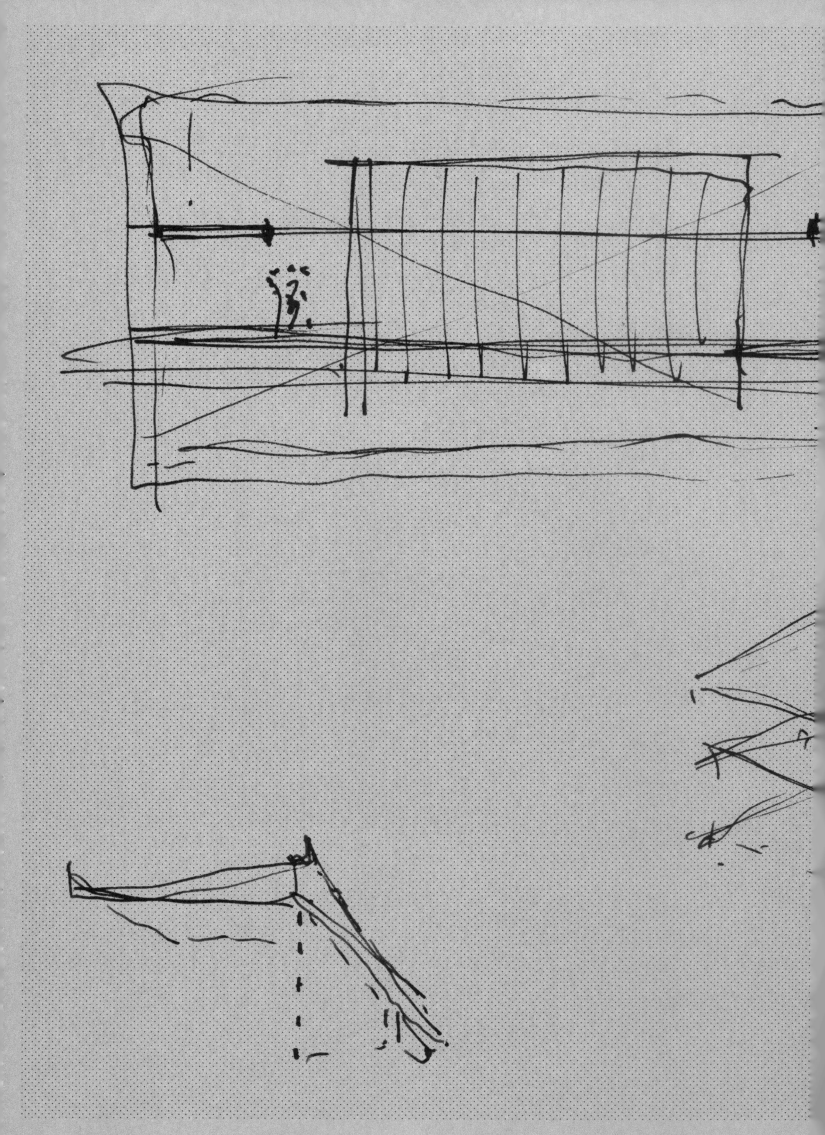

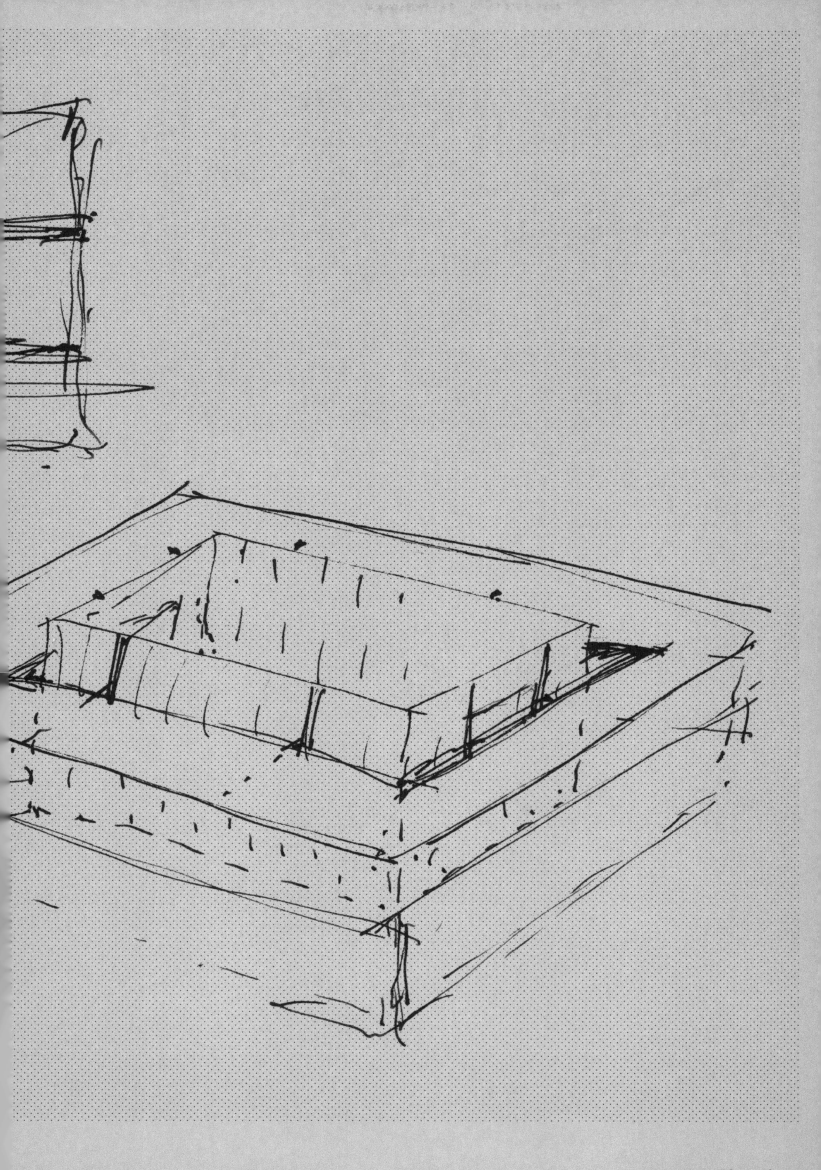

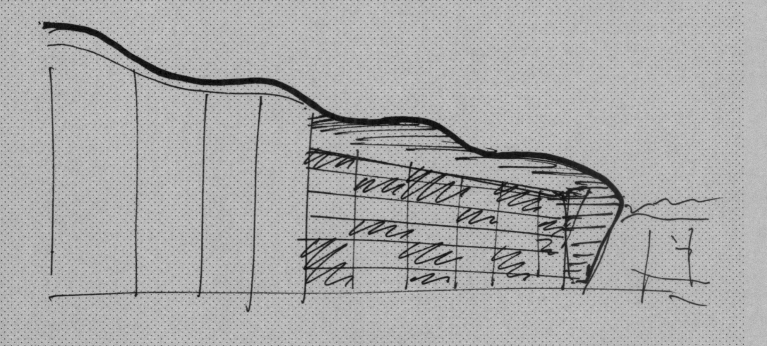

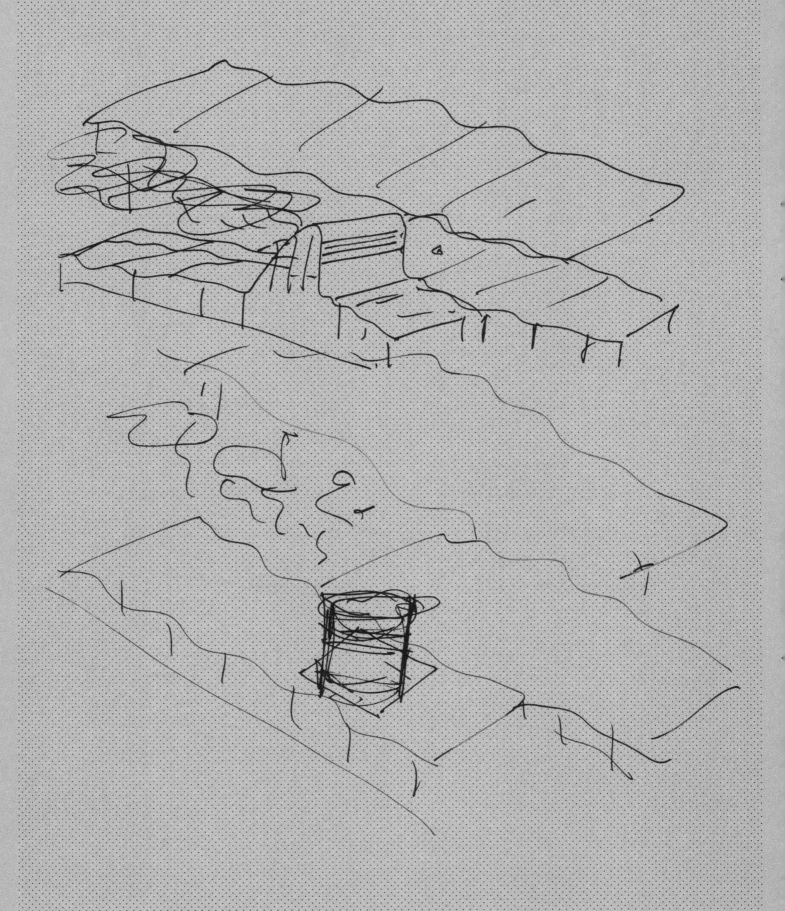

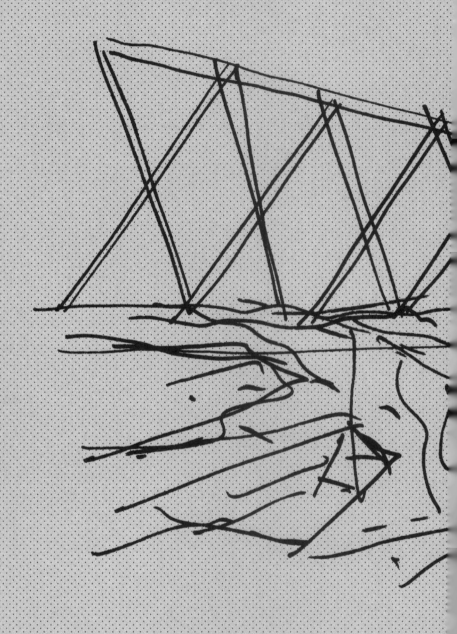

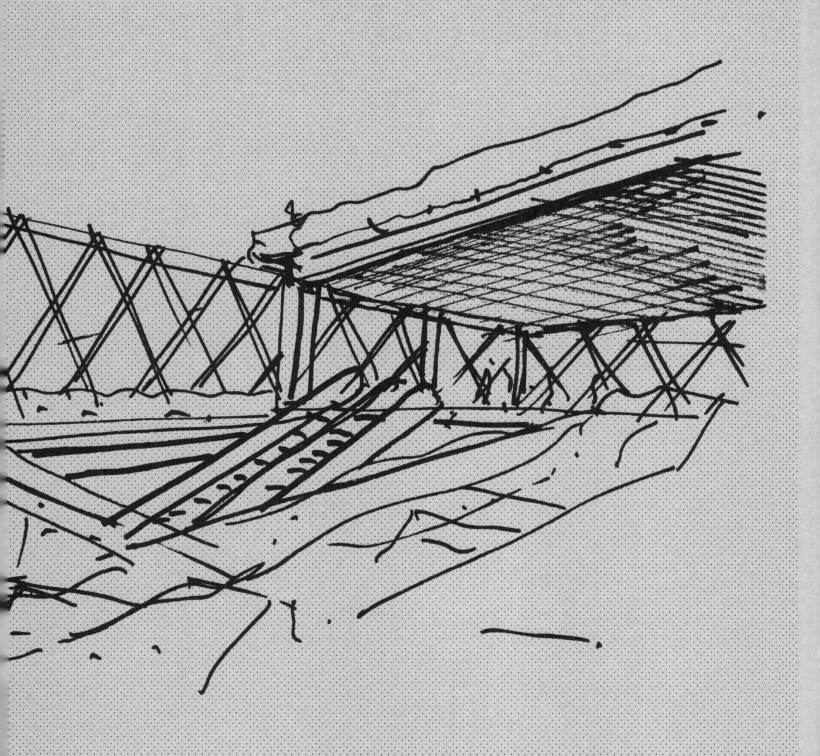

lower level. = rocks.

↓

then proportion.

↓

glass crown.

← "Turkey"
"Karagöz"

'My destiny seemed to be to design bridges', Jacques Ferrier recalls of his student days. As an academic high-flyer, Ferrier had set out to become not an architect but an engineer, enrolling at the highly prestigious École Centrale Paris, the alma mater of, among others, Gustave Eiffel and William LeBaron Jenney (the American designer of what is generally accepted as the world's first skyscraper), not to mention the founders of the great French industrial empires Michelin and Peugeot. But this was not to be. Even as he studied at one of Europe's leading engineering schools, graduating in 1981, Ferrier decided that he wanted to be an architect.

From the beginning, his architectural agenda included a passionate interest in the city. Two books that influenced his thinking were Kevin Lynch's The Image of the City (1960) and Community and Privacy (1964), by Serge Chermayeff and Christopher Alexander. (Another collaborator of Chermayeff's, Alexander Tzonis, was to become a friend and mentor.) But perhaps the greatest influence on the young Ferrier was the British historian and critic Reyner Banham, whose Theory and Design in the First Machine Age (1960) and Architecture of the Well-tempered Environment (1969) offered an optimistic vision of the architecture of the future, rooted in technological advances, which contrasted with the formalism of a Modern Movement in headlong decline. Banham was relatively little read in France, though he was to influence such High Tech masters as Richard Rogers and Norman Foster, in whose office Ferrier would later spend several fruitful years.

When Ferrier enrolled in the architecture school at Paris-Belleville, he found that most of his teachers had little interest in American and British architecture. When the Pompidou Centre, an iconic High Tech landmark, was completed in 1977, the building did not find favour with the French architectural establishment. One of the movement's leaders, the Peruvian-born Henri Ciriani, was a major influence on the school, and the core of his work was a reinterpretation of the canon laid down by Le Corbusier. Under President François Mitterand, from 1981 to 1995, social housing and other public projects remained as the most significant element in the workload of the architectural profession – in stark contrast to Margaret Thatcher's Britain. Mitterand's personal patronage, however, focused on his Grands Projets, which led to commissions for both foreign architects (I.M. Pei, Carlos Ott and J.O. von Spreckelsen) and a new breed of French practitioners (Christian de Portzamparc, Jean Nouvel and Dominique Perrault). Nouvel and Perrault's work reflected High Tech influences, but were also rooted in the French tradition of building in metal and glass, which included the oeuvre of that great constructeur (and chairman of the jury for the Pompidou competition) Jean Prouvé, who was to become a significant influence on Ferrier's architecture.

At the age of twenty-eight, a qualified architect with an agenda that combined an interest in technology with a concern for the social context of design, Ferrier resolved to progress his career beyond France. London beckoned, and he applied for posts at a number of practices with a High Tech bent, including Arup Associates and Nicholas Grimshaw. In the end, however, he was taken on by Foster Associates (as the practice was then known). Norman Foster had been responsible for several outstanding projects in Britain during the 1970s, from the Willis Building in Ipswich to the Sainsbury Centre in Norwich, but the completion of the Hong Kong and Shanghai Bank Headquarters in 1986 established him on the global stage. Spencer de Grey, the director at Foster who hired Ferrier, suggested that he should join the team working on the Carré d'Art arts

01

02

centre in Nîmes, in southern France. Ferrier, however, was not anxious to be despatched back to France, and instead began work on the new terminal building at Stansted Airport. While working in Foster's office, Ferrier discovered the work of Buckminster Fuller and the experimental British practice Archigram, which had influenced Richard Rogers and Renzo Piano's design for the Pompidou Centre. The Foster office at the time was not the mega-practice it has since become (there were no more than seventy people working there at the time), but it benefited from the personal involvement of Norman Foster in virtually all of its projects.

Foster remains something of an inspiration for Ferrier; one critic has even described the latter as 'almost a British architect'. Upon his return to Paris in 1990, Ferrier began to develop a highly individual approach to architecture that certainly owed something to the High Tech tradition, rejecting the formalism of the previous generation of French architects, and responding to functional needs but using technology to create better spaces for people. In some respects, Ferrier is a very French architect. He notes the reluctance of the 'Anglo-Saxons', driven by a pragmatic programme, to engage in a debate about the broader ends of architecture. It would be hard to imagine a British practice with the input that philosopher and writer Philippe Simay provides for the Ferrier atelier. Simay is a partner in the Sensual City Studio, set up by Ferrier and Pauline Marchetti in 2011, and deliberately located a little distance from the practice's office. Both sketching and verbal discussion are part of the formative process of each project: there are no preconceptions, no house style. Once back in France, Ferrier rented a small office in the Bastille quarter and entered into an informal partnership (which ended in 1993) with a friend. He wrote regularly for L'Architecture d'aujourd'hui, developed a special interest in industrial buildings (he had published a book on factory buildings, featuring the work of Foster and Rogers, among others, in 1987) and entered a number of competitions. Following two successful entries in 1990, his independent practice took off.

The first of these, undertaken in association with François Gruson, was for a research centre for MINES Paris Tech, the highly prestigious engineering school founded by Louis XVI in 1783, often known simply as Les Mines but officially the École Nationale Supérieure des Mines de Paris 01 . The historic home of the school is on boulevard Saint-Michel in central Paris, close to the Jardin du Luxembourg. The research centre was to be located some 25 km (16 miles) away to the south, in Évry, a new town developed in the 1960s. The brief called for the accommodation of three distinct departments, and the budget was modest; the building had to be cheap and solid, with no superfluous 'frills'. The industrial aesthetic generated by these prescriptions was in tune with Ferrier's own taste for the functional and straightforward — Foster's Reliance Controls factory (1967), in Swindon, England, was one precedent he had in mind. The plan of the building, with three separate wings divided by garden courts and the circulation made very explicit, is certainly highly rational. Glazed bridges are a striking feature. Beyond the functional response to a practical brief, however, there was a desire to create a workplace that was recognizably a community, with views across the courtyards to provide the necessary connections and an open terrace fronting the library.

The second competition win that established Ferrier's practice was for the Sagep Water Treatment Plant at Joinville-le-Pont 02 , southeast of Paris. The first plant on the site was established in the mid-nineteenth century to draw water from the Marne river to supply the city. Existing filter beds and other structures were to be retained as part of the development. The scale of the operation is impressive: the plant filters around

03

04

05

400,000 m³ (14,125,865 cubic ft) of water daily, enough to supply a third of the needs of Paris. Ferrier's complex of buildings forms the container for what he describes as a 'cathedral of pipes'. The buildings are arranged to a linear diagram, which reflects the processes they house. Generous natural light provides the setting for the gleaming machinery; very few people are required to operate the plant. Externally, the buildings are clad in panels of pre-cast concrete, tinted blue by the addition of cobalt and highly polished. Completed in 1998, the buildings have aged well; indeed, the external concrete panels show little evidence of weathering. The project, another collaboration with François Gruson, is a true rediscovery of the nineteenth-century 'functional tradition' of industrial building.

The Sagep project took some time to move from design to construction. There were several difficult years when new commissions failed to materialize, and Ferrier took up a teaching post at the school of architecture in Saint-Étienne, near Lyon. Teaching has always been important to Ferrier, and he later taught at the École Nationale Supérieure d'Architecture de Bretagne for more than a decade. In 1995 a new project came to the office: a research centre at the Sophia Antipolis science park for the state-funded Inria organization 03, which promotes research and development in the computer and IT industries. The site for the building, an addition to Inria's existing complex, sloped quite steeply; the context was altogether more interesting than that of the practice's first two completed projects. Ferrier felt that the designs should respond to the site and have something of a 'southern' character. A limited use of local stone as cladding on the end elevations was clearly a response to context.

Ferrier describes the building, raised above the ground on pilotis and entered at top-floor level, as 'rational but contextual'. The use of stone was a novel move, but in other respects the project reflected his quest for clear articulation, the effective use of natural light and the creation of social space for a working community. The building was constructed using thick slab floors and columns, with no beams. Ceilings were left as exposed concrete. A precedent that came to mind when Ferrier was working on the designs was Jean Prouvé's house at Nancy (1954), which also occupies a sloping site and is entered at the top of a steep slope. Prouvé's work has been a perennial interest, and his designs perfectly embody the marriage of technology and humanity that Ferrier strives for in his own work. It is, Ferrier says, deeply sensual and poetic in essence, as well as rational. (In 2001, Ferrier was responsible for the design of a major exhibition in Prouvé's hometown of Nancy 04: 'It took up a year of my life,' he recalls, 'but it was a process of rediscovery.')

The key themes that were to drive Ferrier's architecture into the new century were further explored in his designs for the Isomer laboratories (1997–9), in Nantes 05. Here, there was also a strong emphasis on clearly expressed circulation and the manipulation of natural light. The site was close to the Atlantic Ocean, which posed its own challenges in terms of climatic control. The building features a double-skin, a regular feature in Ferrier's work, with external panels of translucent plastic to baffle the wind and rain and protect the inner skin of exposed concrete. The structural strategy echoed that of the Inria project: thick concrete slab floors and columns, with no beams. Inside, the use of colour is bold and the circulation spaces are generous, with loggias as focal points for interaction.

Ferrier's practice established a reputation in the first decade of its existence for an expertise in the design of industrial and laboratory buildings. It was able to respond to highly demanding technical briefs and yet infuse the buildings with an element of humanity, even enjoyment, which makes them good places in which to work. The Modern Movement

06

07

08

09

gloried in technological advance, but the new modernism is about making technology work for people. For Ferrier, it is a matter of re-imagining the role of the architect in society. His modernism is open and versatile, responding to the needs of the buildings' users and context. Another laboratory project, at Oullins, on the outskirts of Lyon, seemed to reflect a new direction in the practice's aesthetic. The site for the Inter Regional Laboratories 06 was in a former industrial zone. When work on the project began in 1998, the area was still littered with the remains of industry in the form of empty buildings and derelict land. Its location, close to the autoroute, was a catalyst for change and regeneration, and today it has been transformed. Ferrier's use of brick as a cladding material was a nod to the local industrial aesthetic. The complex takes the form of three strips of laboratory and office accommodation, separated by gardens. The office wing features an enclosing screen that baffles sunlight and provides a temperate environment within the working spaces.

The contextual theme was further developed in the offices for Total Energie 07, a company that manufactures photovoltaic cells for the generation of power, in Tour-de-Salvagny, near Lyon. The site was in a developing business park, close to open country, and the project took inspiration from the simple barns nearby. The client wanted a building that incorporated offices and production/warehousing space, reflected the 'green' values of the business and was both straightforward and modest in cost. The structure is simple: steel portal frames, spanning 12 m (39 ft) on a 6 m (20 ft) grid and providing flexible, column-free spaces, with façades and roof clad in profiled steel sheeting with timber cladding on the end walls. The building is set into a hillside, with the main entry point at the level of a footbridge that connects the production/warehouse wings with the offices. The project more than met the client's energy-efficiency brief through the use of insulation, photovoltaic cells, reversible heat pumps and the reuse of grey water. Architecturally, it has an elegance that transcends the purely functional: there is nothing spartan about its aesthetic. The success of the project led to a further commission from the same client, a production building in Toulouse 08, completed in 2006. Both projects established Ferrier as an architect able to address issues of sustainability while producing buildings of distinctive form.

The progression of technical and industrial projects on out-of-town sites was punctuated in 2000 by a commission for a substantial office building for Paris's transport authority, RATP, in the 20th arrondissement 09. The urban context is mixed and not particularly distinguished. The architectural treatment of the five-storey building is highly rational and disciplined. Inside, it provides a mix of open plan and cellular offices with a cafeteria and other social spaces for staff. What is uncommon about the building is its provision of natural ventilation via full-height doors, which provide access to generous terraces set behind an outer layer of glazing, a double-skin that provides some respite from the urban noise. The strategy is equally about giving the users of the building more control over their working environment. Yet again Ferrier's concern for making technology work for people emerges strongly.

Ferrier's work over the past decade has developed themes that have preoccupied him from the earliest years of his practice, while applying them to an ever-wider range of contexts, in France and beyond. The Home of Humanities/Marcel Saupin project in Nantes 10, completed in 2009, involved collaboration with several other practices on a major university-led development for a site on the banks of the Loire. Incorporating an existing sports stadium, the scheme includes teaching and residential accommodation, as well as a hotel and offices. Its sheer scale guaranteed

10

11

that it would be controversial, as was the demolition of most of the Stade Marcel-Saupin, a concrete structure from the 1930s that had been the home of FC Nantes until 1984. (The field and one of the stands were retained; Nantes' reserve team still plays there.) The new development is big, bold and colourful, with a glazed double-skin that reflects the light playing on the river.

Ferrier's willingness to engage with large-scale urban development is reflected in two big residential schemes in Montpellier: Mantilla Ilôt 11 and Dominium, both of which feature the use of high-performance concrete, whose whiteness gives the buildings their distinctly Mediterranean look. Ferrier's own origins lie in southern France, and several recent projects have reflected a particular empathy for the landscape and climate of the Midi. The competition scheme for the new Odysseum station on the outskirts of Montpellier 12, which will serve a new fast TGV route that bypasses the city centre, aimed to produce a building with a Mediterranean feel that would be a landmark for a new railway age, just as the Gare de Lyon in Paris or Santa Maria Novella in Florence were expressions of earlier eras of travel. This would be an open, fluid structure, a great metal and glass shed, designed to cope with the southern climate: a twenty-first-century reinterpretation of the great train sheds of the nineteenth century. A naturally ventilated, shaded double-skin, filtering controlled daylight into the interior of the station, was part of the progressive environmental agenda.

Ferrier's competition-winning scheme for a new passenger terminal for the port of Sète 13 also addressed the issue of integrating transport infrastructure into the city. The terminal is the gateway to the Mediterranean and is also a point of arrival. The port had been detached from the life of the city, and the terminal project was in no small measure about reconnecting them. It was conceived not only as a place of passage, but also as an amenity for the inhabitants of the city and a response to its dramatic site, below Mont St-Clair. A new elevated, tree-lined terrace connects city and port and leads directly into the terminal. A restaurant, elevated 20 m (66 ft) above the ground, provides spectacular views; at night it resembles a lighthouse, signalling the haven of the port.

But it is in the area of tall buildings that Ferrier has developed a distinct approach to working in a city where building high has generated intense controversy. (The Tour Montparnasse, begun in 1969, is often cited as the worst blot on the skyline of Paris.) Ferrier's Hypergreen Tower 14 was not designed with Paris, or any other location, in mind. The project, launched in 2005, was about nothing more than reinventing the tall building and creating a highly innovative 'environmental skyscraper', 250 m (820 ft) and sixty storeys high, which would be highly economical in its construction materials, energy consumption and running costs. A key feature was the use of a double-skin; here, it was to be constructed as an external load-bearing lattice of high-performance concrete, developed in consultation with structural engineer Jean-Marc Weill of C & E Ingénierie and manufacturer Lafarge. The performance of the Ductal concrete was comparable to that of steel, and allowed the development of what Weill describes as 'a giant kit in reinforced concrete, made up of pieces that are assembled by post-stressing'.

A gap of 1 m (3 ft) between the outer skin and the façade of the building was an essential factor in the agenda of flexibility and change that drove the project; the structure would be completely independent of the internal plan and façade. This also had practical advantages, in providing accommodation for cleaning cradles, for example, as well as acting as a sun screen. The Hypergreen Tower was conceived as a mixed-use

12

13

38

development that could include offices, housing, a hotel and retailing. The recycling of rainwater and the use of solar collectors, wind turbines and other devices made the tower, if not totally autonomous in terms of its energy needs, a remarkably progressive project. (Indeed, as Ferrier insists, the 'self-sufficient' tower is a myth: tall buildings must take their place in the social, as well as the physical, fabric of the city.) Ferrier sees it as representing a third generation of tall buildings, moving on from the expressive and decorative theme seen in the Chrysler and Empire State buildings in New York, from the 1920s, and the universalism of the Miesian slab, seen to perfection in the Seagram Building, completed in 1958. The project exemplified the marriage of practice and research that has driven the office from its origins.

In practical terms, the Hypergreen project fed into the unbuilt scheme for a 324 m (1,063 ft)-tall office building in the La Défense business quarter, close to J.O. von Spreckelsen's Grande Arche and the Jean Prouvé-engineered CNIT convention centre. An external lattice, climatic as well as structural in function, was again a key feature of the design. The white lattice was drawn more tightly from north to south, to provide protection from solar gain, and opened up to accommodate two levels of terraced gardens, or sky lobbies, intended as places for social interaction with meeting rooms, a bar or a fitness centre. The building would be topped by several levels of restaurants and a business club. By elevating the tower above the ground, Ferrier offered the potential for creating a new public and circulation space, with the landscape passing through the building and the continuity of the city unimpaired. Wind turbines, photovoltaic cells and water recycling were, as at Hypergreen, elements in a low-energy services agenda. The project remained unbuilt, as did Thom Mayne's competition-winning design, but Ferrier remains convinced that high buildings have their place in a city of the future, even Paris. 'The problem with the tower block is not so much its height as its complete alienation from the public space,' he says. 'We must begin to envisage tower blocks rooted in the urban fabric and participating in city life.'

p. 101

A new element of expressiveness in Ferrier's architecture is reflected in the tram-maintenance depot for the city of Bordeaux [A], commissioned in 2003 as part of the city's new tramway system and formally inaugurated at the end of that year. The site was in the Bastide quarter, across the Garonne river from the city centre, for centuries a place of factories and warehouses but in recent years the subject of an ambitious regeneration programme. Ferrier's designs make reference to the 'functional tradition' of the nineteenth century, but equally have a flair that responds to a client's aspirations and is entirely contemporary. The structure is extremely economical, with slender, inverted 'V' columns supporting an undulating roof clad in copper. Transparency and the use of natural light are other important features of this very large building: at night, its opaque glass façades positively glow.

p. 113

The depot was one of many projects, involving a bevy of French and foreign architectural practices, which have made Bordeaux, long regarded as a faded provincial city, a showcase for new architecture. The Breton port of Lorient has also undergone regeneration in recent years. The city was almost entirely destroyed during the Second World War. Ironically, the bombers' key target, the German U-boat base on the Keroman peninsula, survived almost undamaged and today is a tourist attraction. Ferrier's Éric-Tabarly Sailing Museum [B], named for the great Breton yachtsman, occupies a site immediately adjacent to the massive concrete structure that wartime bombs could not destroy. Ferrier's building provides a deliberate contrast in its lightness and

14

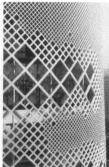

openness to sea views, capitalizing on its location. As well as a base for sailing classes, the building houses exhibitions and a restaurant. The design strategy focused on sustainability and energy efficiency, and paid homage to the shipbuilding tradition of the port of Lorient. The curvaceous form of the structure makes it a landmark on the waterfront, while inside the use of timber boarding for the ceilings is an obvious nautical reference.

p. 157

Regeneration was also the driver for a bridge at Choisy $\boxed{F}$, in the southeastern suburbs of Paris. The area is far from glamorous and the former port area, with its remnants of long-gone industries, was isolated between the Seine and the great swathe of railway tracks carrying the RER. The new bridge, completed in 2010, has opened up the area to new development. Featuring a clear span, without intermediate supports, the bridge is structurally straightforward but given a powerful presence by the wrapping of its structure in a perforated aluminium grid, illuminated a ghostly green by night. Ferrier cites the temporary 'wrapping' of the Pont Neuf, in Paris, by Christo and Jeanne-Claude in 1985 as one of his inspirations for the project, which reflects his desire to make cities more enjoyable, sensual places. It is a modest contribution to the creation of what he describes as 'the sensual city'.

p. 179

The concept was fundamental to the thinking behind the French Pavilion at the Shanghai Expo 2010 $\boxed{H}$, the project that firmly established Ferrier on the global scene. His encounters with the fast-growing cities of the Far East triggered the idea of the sensual city: Shanghai, in particular, seemed to be 'a crucible, distilling the essence of urban society to come'. After winning the competition in 2009, Ferrier's team, led by Pauline Marchetti and Philippe Simay, organized a conference at the Collège de France during which architects, artists, philosophers and historians considered the impact of the senses on architecture and urban design. The Sensual City Studio, established in 2011 by Ferrier and Marchetti as 'a laboratory of ideas, creativity and urban development', was a product of this symposium. Both an independent entity and a think-tank, it has, says Ferrier, 'a vital role in questioning the way we do things'.

The studio has 'a laboratory mindset', but its collaborations with the practice extend beyond the purely speculative. The idea of the 'sensual station' is one product, the central idea behind Ferrier's winning concept in 2012 for the Greater Paris Express scheme $\boxed{15}$, set to produce fifty-seven new rail stations over the next twenty years and in the process redefine Paris as a city that is not confined within the Périphérique. The project is based on the principle of 'shared ambiances and sensory experiences', rather than any overriding architectural prescription. The new stations will 'provide living spaces and interchange points that have a continuous link to the city, delivering new forms of communal living; businesses and services, artistic expression and cultural encounters will all have their place.' The fact that both the SGP, the organization responsible for the scheme, and the RATP, the Paris transport authority, have embraced this radical vision is remarkable.

The French Pavilion set the agenda for the collaboration between office and studio and for the emerging concept of the sensual city. Having won the design competition from a field of forty-nine entrants, the practice was responsible for both the building and its contents, so that visitors could enjoy 'a real architectural experience, where the content and the container are integral parts of a single universe.' Ferrier describes the pavilion as 'in some ways, a "built" research project'. Working again with Jean-Marc Weill, a key collaborator of the practice, he evolved a design for a building that appears to float above the surrounding pool

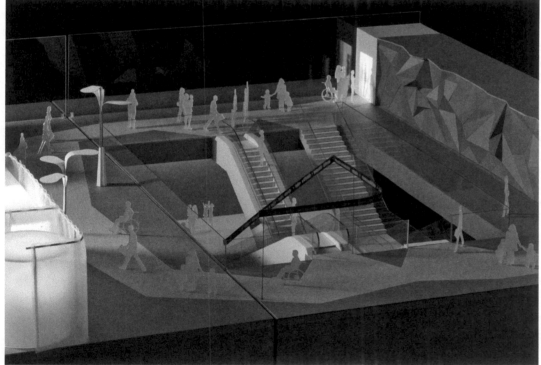

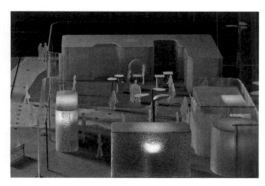

15

of water. A flexible container is contained within a cross-braced mesh that has the appearance of concrete, but is in fact fabricated of steel, clad in glass-reinforced plastic. Its 'doughnut' plan wraps display and other spaces around a central garden court, with the roof of the building formally planted in the classical French manner associated with André Le Nôtre, the seventeenth-century landscape architect behind Versailles and Vaux-le-Vicomte. The design of the gardens by Agence TER was calculated to reinforce the sensory experience fundamental to Ferrier's vision. The pavilion was an inspired response to the agenda set by the theme of the Expo: 'Better City, Better Life'. For Ferrier, it was an opportunity 'to found a ground-breaking link between project and technology, and thus reveal new uses for the future city.' Uniquely among the national pavilions, it was retained and converted for use as a contemporary art museum, a reflection of its popularity with visitors and the people of Shanghai.

p. 123

The project reflected Ferrier's desire to underpin practice with a serious commitment to research and experiment, and to combine pragmatism with a more idealistic agenda. The growing range and scale of the practice's workload poses a challenge to his ambition to create buildings that are both functional and beautiful. There was little scope for extravagant gestures in the design for a delivery centre for Airbus on its manufacturing site next to the Toulouse–Blagnac Airport C. Completed in 2006 and formally inaugurated by President Nicolas Sarkozy and the German Chancellor Angela Merkel, it is where airlines collect their aircraft. The centre is on the scale of a small airport, with its own check-in, baggage handling and security provisions. Ferrier remarks that the budget for the project was modest — perhaps 10 per cent of the cost of just one of the aircraft it processes — but the building has a dynamism of form and elegance of detail that expresses something of the excitement of flight. What could Ferrier achieve with a full-scale airport terminal commission?

p. 135

The interaction of experiment and practice has fuelled other recent projects by the team. The use of an external screen, mediating between interior and exterior, has been a recurring theme in Ferrier's architecture, an environmental device with considerable aesthetic potential. A recent example of its use is seen at the offices for champagne firm Piper-Heidsieck D, completed in 2008. The company, founded in 1785, is steeped in tradition, but its decision to move from the centre of Reims to an out-of-town site close to the Champagne-Ardennes TGV station, a forty-minute journey from Gare de l'Est, in Paris, is a reflection of its business ambitions. CEO Anne-Charlotte Amory was an exacting client, demanding a building that provided not only new office space for around sixty staff, but also one that referenced the company's products. The result is a 2,000 m² (21,528 sq ft) building, essentially a glazed container with four two-storey pavilions, within a mesh of metal screening, which sparkles by day and glows by night. The external metal screen, using four laser-cut panel patterns, makes reference to the 'cages' used to store champagne bottles and to the sparkling character of the wine. Inside, detailing is crisp and minimal, with an emphasis on the subtle use of controlled natural light. The success of the project led to a commission for a further phase of development, underway in 2014–15.

p. 147

The Piper-Heidsieck project clearly benefited from the involvement of a strongly motivated client with clear objectives. In contrast, an office development in Grenoble E, a city with a strong 'green' agenda, was designed for a developer working within a masterplan set by the city council. The site was immediately adjacent to the Autoroute de Suisse, hence the desire to see a building of some quality there. The use of a perforated screen to shade the façade is again a key feature, repeated in the Les Yeux

16

p. 167

Verts multi-storey car park in Soissons [G]. The functional steel and concrete structure of the building is partly concealed by a cladding formed of spruce panels, which have been applied at a variety of angles and relieved by areas of planting. Internally, large photographic images are used to identify the different levels, a playful but practical device inspired by Charles and Ray Eames' design for their picture-card deck, House of Cards (ill. p. 81). Ferrier uses the device of a multilayered façade in very different contexts. For the Sulwhasoo flagship store in Hong Kong [16], for example, he succeeded in creating a sense of depth in the very narrow space allowed by local planning regulations.

p. 205

Ferrier today remains firmly rooted in Paris. The recently completed headquarters for the French publisher Hachette [J] is located, significantly, just outside the Périphérique and is a marker in the regeneration of a neglected quarter of the city. But today the practice works on an international scale, with a number of projects in China. Ferrier has doubts about the impact of 'iconic' Western architects on the fast-developing cities of the East, concerned about the relevance of architecture if it is only about producing one-off, prestige-object buildings. On the other hand, he is a perennial optimist, seeing the changing global scene and the emergence of new economic super powers in, for instance, India and Brazil, as a catalyst for the reinvention of the architect. Reinventing the modernist tradition is at the core of Ferrier's work; it is a process to which he is set to make a major contribution in the decades to come.

The Architecture of Jacques Ferrier

KP   Perhaps we could start by going back to your earliest years: your education, your formative experience as an architect, your inspirations, the figures who inspired you. What architects and designers helped you to forge your own approach to architecture? Where does it come from, in other words?

    JF   When I was at the École Centrale Paris, I was destined to build bridges, but I was interested in architecture. During my studies there I ended up studying it in a rather self-taught way, by browsing in a specialist architecture bookshop. The first works I chose (which weren't part of the culture of French architecture schools at the time) were Community and Privacy by Serge Chermayeff and Christopher Alexander, and The Image of a City, by Kevin Lynch. But Reyner Banham was really the greatest influence.

    After graduating, we started a magazine, Dépliant, with a group of friends, dedicated to the major figures of the 1960s and '70s. We published a full translation of 'The Missing Motel', an article by Reyner Banham that was not available in French at the time. I was also fascinated by Charles and Ray Eames and their ability to work on different kinds of elements: toys, furniture, movies, books and buildings. Since then, I have always kept their House of Cards picture-card deck by my side.

KP   What was the significance of Banham and these other writers for you?

    JF   When I began my architectural training, I realized that the culture in architecture schools was very different from the culture I'd begun to discover through these books. In France at the time (this was in 1985), there was a mix of post-Le Corbusier, what we might call neo-modern, as well as a rapidly growing awareness of social issues. It was either post-Le Corbusier or sociological. These were the two main trends.

    So I arrived with a background that was a mix of British and American theories from the 1960s, which were somewhat ignored in France. But, as luck would have it, there was a lecturer who took me under his wing and didn't discourage me from pursuing these interests. He was a Frenchman named François Laisney, who essentially said, 'It's strange that your interests should lean in that direction, but why not?' And he let me continue exploring this avenue during my studies.

KP   But High Tech did come to France with Pompidou…

    JF   Yes, High Tech arrived with the Pompidou Centre in the 1970s. But that was a very isolated example at the time, and even today, in French architectural culture. And indeed, you can see that there have been no other buildings in France inspired by the Pompidou Centre.

KP   So it was a one-off?

    JF   Yes, it was a one-off. And what I'm producing now is also very much in a different direction.

KP   When did you join Norman Foster's office?

    JF   In 1987. With my training, I was very interested in the British architectural scene. And Richard Rogers and Foster were, in a way, companions of Reyner Banham. So it was with this in mind that I applied for posts at Arup, Grimshaw, Rogers and Foster. In the end, it was Foster who offered me a job. When I went for an interview, Spencer de Grey said to me, 'You're French, you can work on the Nîmes project,' as Foster had been commissioned to build the Carré d'Art in Nîmes. I said no, because I wanted to work in London; I didn't want to go back to France. And it wasn't just France, but the south of France, close to where I was born, so I was even less inclined to go back! Spencer, who was the second-in-command at the firm, was very surprised to have someone refuse a job, and a few days later called me back and said, 'We've found you a different project. You can work on Stansted Airport.' So that was a good experience. It was at Foster Associates that I truly learned what it was to work in an architectural practice, at a time when the Great Portland Street office still comprised just seventy people. It was there that I discovered the works of Buckminster Fuller; he was a key influence on Foster. Later, I distanced myself from his work, but this was a time when I was very enthusiastic about his highly technological vision of the world.

50

KP There was, in a way, a different tradition in France with Jean Prouvé. When you were an architecture student, was Prouvé highly rated in France? You designed an exhibition of his work. Was that part of a process of rediscovery?

JF His image was that of an engineer who collaborated on architectural projects. It was only later, after I'd qualified, that I came across his name in several books I was reading, and much later, when I was in charge of designing the exhibition for the 100th anniversary of his birth in 2001, that I gained a more comprehensive vision of his work and influence, and his importance to me, personally.

KP And because the people who were interested in Prouvé were the High Tech people, weren't they?

JF I think that those who were interested in Prouvé in France weren't at the forefront of the architectural scene. At the time, Renzo Piano or Richard Rogers cited Prouvé much more than any French architect.

KP We've talked about French architecture when you were a student and just starting out, but how has your work developed since? How does your work stand apart from the mainstream? Three particularly well-known French architects are Nouvel, Portzamparc and Perrault: is there a common theme in their work? Where does the French architectural centre today lie? Is your own work French, or is it international? Is it High Tech in a British tradition?

JF There is a very long Beaux-Arts tradition in French architecture, and what we call neo-modernism was a very formalistic interpretation of the work of Le Corbusier. I see in this neo-Le Corbusier movement something quite fixed and rigid that I don't see when I visit his Unité d'Habitation, in Marseille. For me, it's very humanistic, sensual and inventive. It doesn't fit in with the kind of academicism of these neo-modern architects. At the other end of the spectrum is Jean Nouvel, who was the leading figure of the French architectural scene during the 1980s and '90s, the period when he was truly creative. You can see that he displays a total disinterest in the technological side of things. He puts in place something that runs counter to modernist academicism, but is also, in common with this tradition, very formal and not at all rooted in technology.

I found myself in an architectural scene dominated by two opposing kinds of formalism. What really interested me was the relationship between technology and society. When I set up my own practice, I immediately saw that I might not have the opportunities of Foster or Rogers, who were working on prestigious projects and were in a position to use costly cutting-edge technology. In this constraint, however, I saw an avenue to be explored, namely working on the relationship between people and technology, but on an everyday level, using quite ordinary technology. It was possible to adopt an architectural stance that made use of different technologies, even if they weren't at the cutting edge, and work on products straight out of the catalogue. It is in choosing, combining and expertly assembling these ordinary, everyday products that they become more noble.

KP Using ordinary materials, such as galvanized metal, rather than the most expensive materials?

JF Yes. For example, I used corrugated panels on the research laboratories for MINES ParisTech. When the project was underway, the client said to me, 'But this material, it's surely not the same thing that's used in the supermarket I go to every day?' I replied, 'Yes, the very same.' And he said, 'But that's terrible!', to which I replied, 'Ah, but we're going to use it in a different way.' And, indeed, when the building was completed, he said, 'No, it's not possible, it can't be the same product.' But it was, and it was straight out of the same catalogue.

So it was really this idea that I could express myself in a way that wasn't formal, something I've never been comfortable with, but instead by producing buildings and projects that were based on thinking that encompassed both the technologies used and the purposes of the buildings. In this respect, it was fortunate that my first projects were research labs or production facilities. We had to address very precise functional briefs, which steered me safely away from any temptation to stray into formalism.

Interview with Jacques Ferrier

KP   Now that you're working on the global stage, do you find that there is any meaning in national identity in architecture? If architecture is global, does it lose any specific identity and become merely an international, rather faceless kind of process? In China, for example, a building can be built in a month, with mechanized production. How do your values count in this kind of scene?

JF   When we respond to a project abroad — particularly in China, where we have had the greatest number of projects since the French Pavilion at Shanghai Expo 2010 — I address it by taking this non-formal approach. I don't come to a project with the idea that I'm going to produce buildings that are round or square, but rather with this method that we've talked about, where I pay a great deal of attention to uses and technology. Today, I add to this a sensitivity to geography, climate and culture, and to local influences. So I'm an international architect, but when I arrive in a country, in another culture, the first thing I do is read books, travel around the city and get a feel for its atmosphere. What I try to achieve is what I call a 'mutual gaze', so that although I'm an architect rooted in French culture, I am also able to come to a project attentive, porous and receptive to another one. What I try to put forward is an architecture that is clearly mine, but is influenced by context – in the same way that if I were to build in northern France or southern France, the result would be different.

KP   How does this approach contrast with the work of, say, Zaha Hadid or Frank Gehry?

JF   The international style of Mies van der Rohe has been replaced, in a way, by the international style of branding favoured by a dozen or so big-name architects. So while the work of architects such as Hadid or Gehry is obviously very different from that of Mies, in some way there is always this philosophy, this idea, that architectural projects are indifferent to the place in which they are built. I think that the future of architecture today, which will no doubt feature growing numbers of young architects from India, China, Europe and South America, will be about architecture that responds to context, not in a regressive or nostalgic way, but taking into account different construction cultures and interaction with places.

KP   It's pretty obvious your work has always rejected the idea of arbitrary form, creating something that's memorable just for the sake of its look.

JF   I'm not at all comfortable with formal intuition. My work often begins with texts and small sketches and a lot of discussion and interaction with the people who work with me at the practice. This is very much a preliminary phase, before any drawings or designs are produced. In that sense, I think, I'm very French. From what I understand about the British approach, people are very wary of discourse, of ideas and intellectual references, at least insofar as architecture is concerned.

KP   That's a very specifically French way of approaching a project.

JF   I think it is very French. But at the other extreme, even when we evoke big ideas, the question of details and materials always very quickly comes into play. So the discussion may be very general, but at the same time we hone in on details, and we might say, for instance, 'Could we make it out of wood, but have the assembly details made out of metal?'

KP   Can we move on to the idea of the sensual city? You've talked about the need, in the light of vast global urban expansion, to create cities that focus not just on functional performance, but also on joy and diversity and space for the individual. How do you achieve this, particularly in the context of growing cities in China, which are mushrooming? Is there any hope that the world city will become a more enjoyable, diverse place, or will it just be multiplied urban sprawls?

JF   In our vision of urban planning and development, the Chinese city has played a major role, or at least Shanghai has, because the Huangpu river divides the city into two parts. On one side is an extremely vibrant mix of skyscrapers, small shops and street vendors, which is full of noise and smells and is busy day and night, but not steeped in nostalgia, as every day a new skyscraper springs up. On the other is Pudong, the new district, which was built almost from scratch barely twenty years ago, based on functional urban plans, and where there isn't the same sort of vibrancy at all. It's soulless, with very wide avenues, and no nightlife. To answer your question, I've seen the

        Interview with Jacques Ferrier

damage that this kind of functional, geometrical urban planning can do. I've seen it in the satellite towns of Singapore, where a very rich economy produces urban environments without any qualities at all. We need to stop producing umpteen carbon copies of the functional city, which is replicated absolutely everywhere, and instead address all five senses and integrate the way in which we perceive the smells and noises of the city, the climate and topography into urban design.

KP   So it comes back to the theme that technology is a neutral thing that can be used beneficially. It's not, as some people see it, about globalized uniformity, with the destruction of local cultures. Can it be used to enhance local cultures?

JF   In the 1950s and '60s, you would have air-conditioning everywhere, but you couldn't open a window. With today's innovative ventilation technologies, you can have air-conditioning and you can also open the window, as when you open it a sensor informs the building's nerve centre that a window is open and stops the air-conditioning. In the springtime in France, for example, by opening a window you can enjoy the scent of lilac, hear the sounds of cars and conversations, and so on. This is what we mean by this idea of the sensual city: buildings, having been hermetically sealed for fifty years, can once again be opened up to the outside world. This brings us back to the idea of context. Buildings can once again benefit from, and interact with, their surroundings.

KP   There's the issue of the importance of philosophical debate in the French scene, which you said is perhaps not very important in the Anglo–American tradition. But your practice has developed a very philosophical approach to architecture, which you believe is able to change the way in which buildings are created and, ultimately, to make better buildings. How does the Sensual City Studio relate to that? Where does it feed in?

JF   Well, after the experience of the French Pavilion for the Shanghai Expo 2010, where we were also in charge of the contents of the pavilion, I said to myself that if we kept the practice as it was, all of these ideas would be lost in the day-to-day production of projects. It was at this point that I had the idea of teaming up with Pauline Marchetti to create the Sensual City Studio, in a different location in Paris.

KP   Is it important that it's in a different place?

JF   Yes, it really was the right decision. It's only two Métro stops away from here – you can walk to it in fifteen minutes – but it's a different atmosphere, especially as we were very quickly joined by a young philosopher, Philippe Simay. And so there is a sense of it being a research laboratory, which interacts with the main practice in order to call into question the way projects are produced.

KP   Obviously, the French Pavilion was a very important step in all this, bringing together the worlds of practice and ideas and the sensual theme...

JF   It was very important in two ways. First, because for two years I went to China every month, which put me directly into contact with the urgency of the global urban scene, far more than one can sense it in Europe. And second, when the question of the contents of the pavilion arose, there was the idea of focusing on sustainable architecture. But we said to ourselves, 'All the pavilions are going to be talking about sustainable architecture,' and I had just curated an exhibition on sustainable architecture at the Pavillon de l'Arsenal. It was then that I realized that this idea of sustainability was going to be the backdrop of every project from now on, and that we would have to go a step further and explain why architecture needs to be sustainable.

KP   Do you ever see a project in a magazine that isn't said to be sustainable? Everyone claims to be sustainable. What does it mean?

JF   Today, you can design a building that looks like a Greek temple, which is, in fact, extremely sustainable. In other words, there is no relationship between a building's form and its sustainability credentials. We decided that we could use the concept of sustainable development to think differently about the role of technology in the city and in buildings, in such a way that we call upon technology to be even more efficient and, at the same time, invisible. The idea is to get back to this idea of urban pleasure and to recognize that, as we all live in megacities now, we need to take care of people and, more specifically, of people's bodies.

                                                                     Interview with Jacques Ferrier

KP   And their souls!

JF   Yes, exactly, and their souls, too.

KP   Not just function, but enjoyment; something deeper.

JF   Yes, and I think that it is linked – and I'd like to emphasize this – not to deindustrialization, but to the miniaturization of technology and the very high performance of new technology. Scientists and those who develop new technology always aim to produce better and ever-more efficient solutions, but they don't really address the question of usage, which is why, in my view, the architect's role is that of an intermediary, or a mediator, between technology and society. As an architect, I'm in a position to ask, for example, if a new product is truly consistent with the vision of urban life that I want to share. That should be the architect's position, not to accept all new technologies, nor to reject them all outright, but to sift through them and put in place things that can contribute to this humanist view of the city we wish to implement today.

KP   That makes the architect's role very important, as a kind of mediator.

JF   Architects can either respond to issues that have a real influence on the life of our society or focus on those that are purely about style and the image of architecture. In that case, the role of the architect will gradually dwindle away and disappear, because it would just be about branding and celebrity. In this respect Brad Pitt would be even more famous than Frank Gehry. And if Brad Pitt were to say, 'Tomorrow, I'm going to design buildings,' every billionaire in Qatar or Abu Dhabi or China will want a Brad Pitt-designed building!

KP   If you went from here, in central Paris, to beyond the Périphérique, you would see miles of buildings, sheds, supermarkets, mass housing, not really architecture at all, or even designed by architects. So the architect could ultimately be reduced to a small number of people doing luxury objects, with the rest of our buildings just thrown up by computers.

JF   That's very much the danger. There's a risk of not being able to see the wood for the trees. I agree that the future for architecture looks bleak, where we have a few very prestigious buildings, such as the Guggenheim museums or skyscrapers, which are dropped in the city like giant Louis Vuitton bags, so the mayor or the minister can say, 'Look! I've got a big Vuitton bag too, just like you!' And consequently the rest of our architectural production — that is, the remaining 99 per cent — could end up being built by contractors or software packages.

KP   Of course, the rejection of the Modern Movement was about rejecting architects, who were seen as creating hideous buildings, destroying cities, making everything uniform. Architects have got to reinvent themselves, which I suppose is why some people started doing funny shapes, so that the public thinks, 'Oh, that's interesting.'

JF   I like this idea of reinventing ourselves. We don't really know what's happening today in South America, in Africa or in India, but I hope, given the urgency of the issues affecting big cities, that there will be people — architects, urbanists, philosophers, designers — who are reinventing themselves in order to respond to this question of an urban society. This is what we are trying to do.

KP   Perhaps we could talk about some of the themes relating to architectural detail. There's the idea of the perforated screen, which is the relationship between a functional object in the middle and what you do around it. Is it purely decorative or is it much bigger than that, as at the offices for Piper-Heidsieck, where the building is contained within this sort of mesh? Is it purely an aesthetic device?

JF   No, it's not just an aesthetic response, and it's true that your question picks up on a very interesting relationship when you say that it's a mediator between an ideal architecture/world and reality. This vision that you have of my work perhaps sums up my experiences with the double-skin façade.

KP   Which is such a constant theme...

JF   It is a response in terms of the building's thermal behaviour, which has enabled me to have façades with larger areas of glazing, as they are protected by external meshes. In addition, it has allowed me to make buildings that are not as expensive, because we

57

can have an extremely simple main façade, as the image of the building comes from the second façade, which can be more sophisticated and more decorative since it doesn't have to be watertight and has no functional role. So, in a way, when it comes to these kinds of projects, in particular office buildings, what I do amounts to isolating the 'technical efficiency' aspect of the façade and resolving it very cheaply with a simple main façade, and then tackling the aesthetic aspect via this second façade, 1 m (3 ft) in front of the first. Incidentally, it isn't easy to convince clients — although we're now more experienced in this regard — that having a double-skin façade of this kind will be cheaper than trying to produce a single, very beautiful 'real' façade.

This strategy has allowed me to respond to the functional requirements and real needs of the building, while at the same time creating an image freed from functional constraints. The outer façade can respond to the question of image and the building's interaction with its surrounding environment. This is very much the case with the offices for Piper-Heidsieck, with this golden façade reflecting the effervescence of champagne.

KP So there's an element of symbolism in the outer façade of the Piper-Heidsieck building, which expresses the product. But it's still a highly functional building. The actual office spaces are high-performance, straightforward and efficient.

JF Exactly. I felt it was necessary to respond to this need for symbolism, but I also felt that the symbolic response should be part and parcel of a process of rational and constructive reflection. That's why it took some time and a few buildings before arriving at an enriching response. Today, I feel that a building is responsible for conveying an image, with respect to the city and the public space. It has taken time to find a response that wasn't formal, but was a continuation of my research into materials and the uses of buildings.

KP So the approach for that project could be further developed in other work, as could this element of symbolism, given the right project?

JF It was clearly developed when the question of the French Pavilion arose. An exhibition pavilion is clearly symbolic, so the answer there was to say that this double-skin façade was also a structure, because, in fact, the idea for the pavilion was that the interior space should be free of all shear walls and just have vertical pillars. This reflects my idea that a contemporary building, in order to last, must be able to transform itself in situ, which is why the bracing structure was moved to the outside. The lattice structure not only creates the building's image, but also holds the building together. Moreover, thanks to this structural device the pavilion hasn't been demolished, but instead has been transformed into a museum of contemporary art. Inside the pavilion, we proposed an additional option, because here, for the first time in one of my projects, the external façade was a green one.

KP Can we talk a little bit about tall buildings? Obviously, Hypergreen is a very important project, and is a good example of the experimental research aspect of the practice and the studio coming together. You haven't yet built a tall building, but is there a thought process behind Hypergreen that will inform future projects?

JF Yes, it was a major milestone, this idea of doing research alongside our competition projects, and in a way it foreshadowed the next step, which was the creation of the Sensual City Studio. With the Hypergreen project, we really wanted to allow ourselves the time and space for a fully fledged, innovative reflection. It was important to have an industrial partnership, and fortunately we were able to forge one with Lafarge, one of the world's leading cement manufacturers, so naturally our thinking leaned towards an innovative concrete structure. For me, this was an opportunity to address what the third generation of skyscrapers might look like. The first generation comprised the stone skyscrapers, beginning in Chicago and ending with the Empire State Building in New York. The second generation, which in my opinion is still today's generation, began in the 1950s with the Seagram Building in New York, and is typified by structures that are designed as very large-scale objects, but are not orientated and, regardless of their shape (pointed, round, square), are typically imagined as shiny, glimmering glass-and-metal envelopes.

Interview with Jacques Ferrier

60

What is interesting about Hypergreen is that there's this idea of a glazed object that has been inserted into a mineral meshwork. And so, with the solidity of the outer structure, we find in the space between the inner façade and this structure the interplay of light, shadow and depth that was to a certain extent present in the first skyscrapers in Chicago and New York.

KP So it's very unusual. If you look at the recent tall buildings by Skidmore Owings & Merrill or Renzo Piano or Richard Rogers, they're largely all steel structures. This use of concrete is very unusual, isn't it?

JF The idea of building 200 m (656 ft) high with a precast concrete structure was made possible by new types of concrete. Today, there are extremely mouldable concretes that are used for high-performance bridges, but could also be used for the structure of this skyscraper project. There are even what are known as ultra-high-performance concretes, which are almost as resilient and durable as steel. The next question raised by Hypergreen was: 'What is the urban role of the tall building?'

We decided to limit the height to around 200 m (656 ft), because that's the maximum height at which you can still open windows. The idea was to invent this new form of natural ventilation, combined with mechanical installations, obviously, but allowing fresh air into the building via natural means. That's why I feel that this height limit is reasonable, and I think it fits in well with the urban skyline. It also means that, in terms of moving around the building, you don't have too many lift changes to make. When you go up the tallest tower in Dubai, the Burj Khalifa, the trip up in the lift is a nightmare: you have to change lifts four times to get to the top. And in terms of the relationship to the city, whether you're at 400 m (1,312 ft) or 600 m (1,969 ft), the view's the same, because you're so far away that what the eye sees is a kind of overview, as if you're on an aeroplane, and you lose the sense of belonging to the city.

Our line of thinking was that a skyscraper of reasonable height, 150 to 200 m (492 to 656 ft), was a good response in terms of creating urban density, and that by freeing up internal space, this external structure was a good base for a mixture of uses, including housing, hotels and offices.

KP That tall-building issue is interesting, isn't it? You can make a tall building that is self-contained, detached from the city. Indeed, there were dreams in the past of tall buildings with everything contained inside, such as Frank Lloyd Wright's unbuilt Mile High Illinois, where you would never need to go outside.

JF I am not in favour of buildings that claim to be completely self-sufficient in terms of energy. I believe that the whole history of a city is based on exchange and interaction, and I prefer the idea of, for example, a housing complex that at night uses the heat produced by the office building next door during the day. There's always this idea of buildings being mutually interdependent, like urban society.

KP The idea of public space is key to your work as consulting architect for the stations of the new Greater Paris Express network, isn't it? I gather it is not about designing the stations themselves, but informing the process of design by involving many architects with a commonality of theme throughout.

JF This was a perfect example of a successful collaboration between the practice and the Sensual City Studio. Our approach was to say that this 'family resemblance' was not going to be in the shapes and forms of the stations, but rather in the passenger experience. So it was important for us to define, in this passenger experience, what is important. We established two broad themes. One was about sensations in terms of acoustic quality, natural light and materiality; in other words, the experience of moving around inside and through the stations. The second was the idea that a metro station is really a public space within the metropolis. For me, public spaces are no longer just the precisely defined public squares of the classic city. If you look at the greater Paris region, there are a lot of designated spaces of this kind that are always empty. By contrast, those places where there's a real expression of community life is where people gravitate towards. Naturally, these places might be shopping centres (which are, in fact, private spaces), but they could also be metro stations and transport hubs,

Interview with Jacques Ferrier

places that people are obliged to pass through and are truly public spaces because they are managed by the community. These are places where there should be service points, retail spaces that truly interact with the city in such a way that there is an intensive community life. We also attached a great deal of importance to the station concourse, as it's the external concourse that establishes the link between the station building and the city. In these spaces, there will be the same trees and street furniture, in order to signal that these are places to wait for a bus, meet a friend, and so on. Unfortunately, this is an idea that has prompted a lot of opposition from some quarters, because people want these kinds of public spaces, but do not want to see people loitering in them.

This brings us back to our discussion of the role of the architect. In a way, the client would like these stations to be just a collection of architecture and, as we only select good architecture firms, the idea is to have high-quality architecture. But for me, this isn't enough, as I'd like this commonality to be the way that architecture interacts with the neighbourhood and with the city. This is especially important in the case of Paris, compared to London or Berlin, say, because the concept of the greater metropolitan area — as opposed to the small city within the Périphérique — has a real image problem and a lack of public urban activity and animation. Personally, I see these new metro lines around the city as an opportunity to finally get it to function like an archipelago, and not as an entity that is always defined in reference to the urban core at its centre. But to achieve this, there needs to be a proper urban project for the areas around each station. Otherwise, we will end up with a tool but no content.

These images refer to two common sources of personal inspiration, confronting and enriching one another: the simple community life of the seaside village of Ferrier's childhood in the south of France, where the urban landscape has been built according to climate and local workmanship; and the fascinating, never-ending complexity of the Asian metropolis, beloved destination of his frequent trips to the Far East.

A

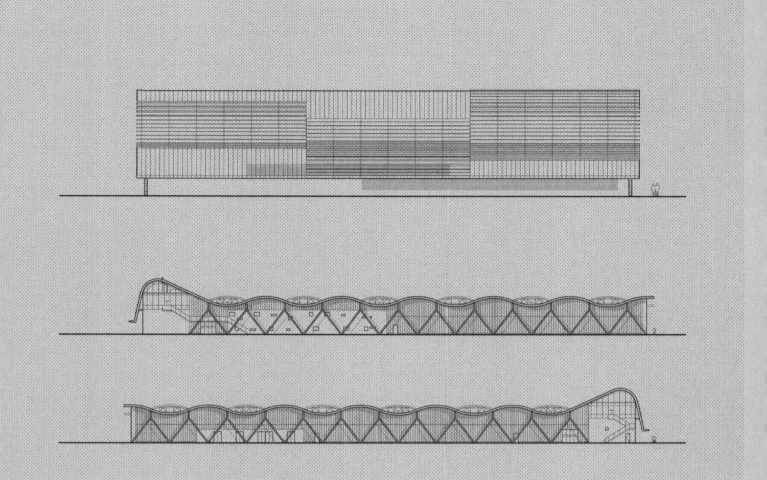

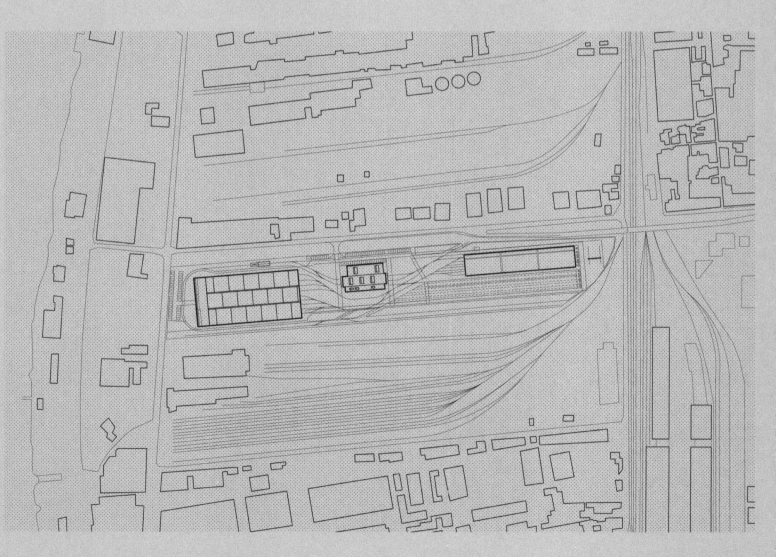

1:500

1:1000

1:2500

B

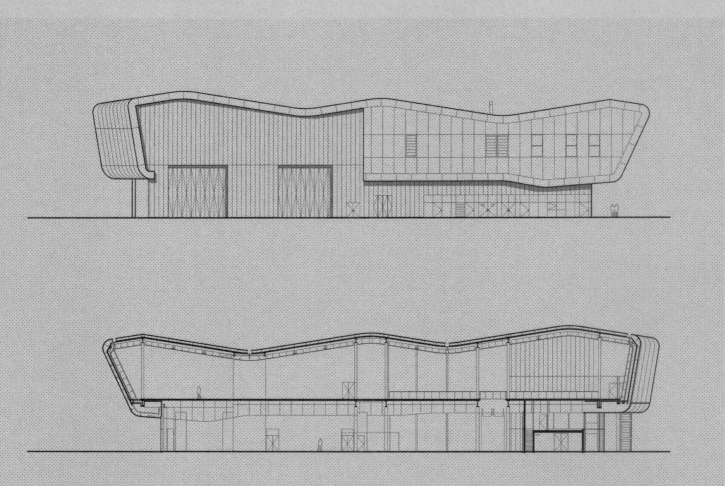

1:500

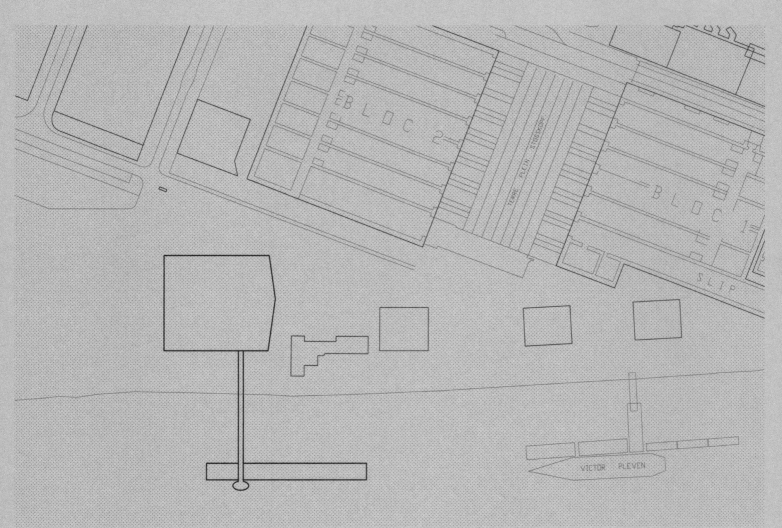

1:2500

1:500

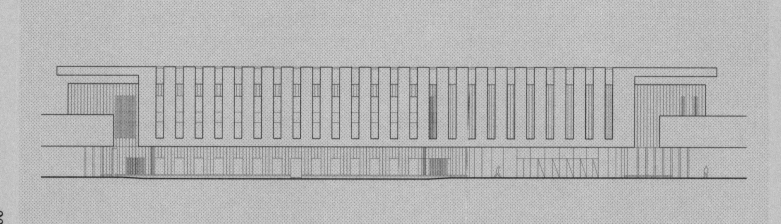

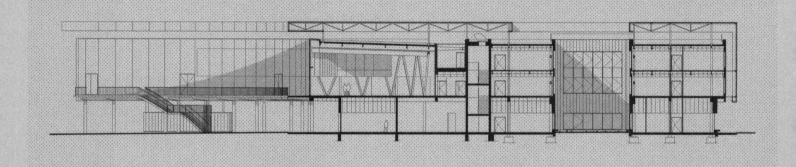

1:2500

D

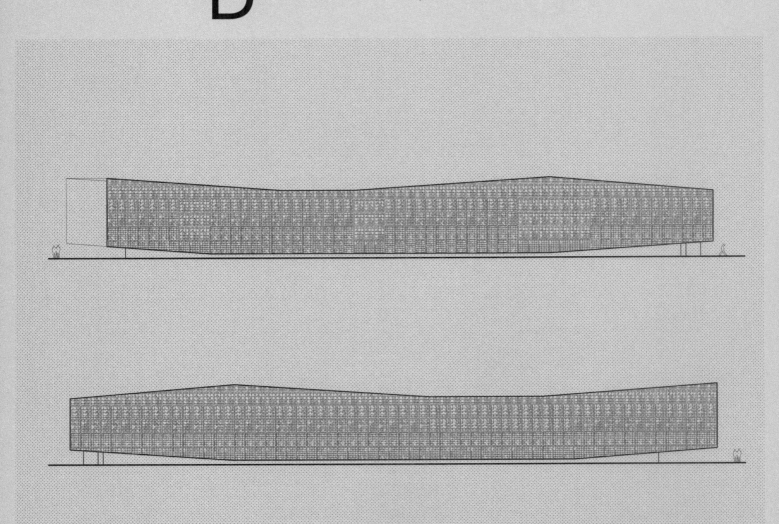

1:500

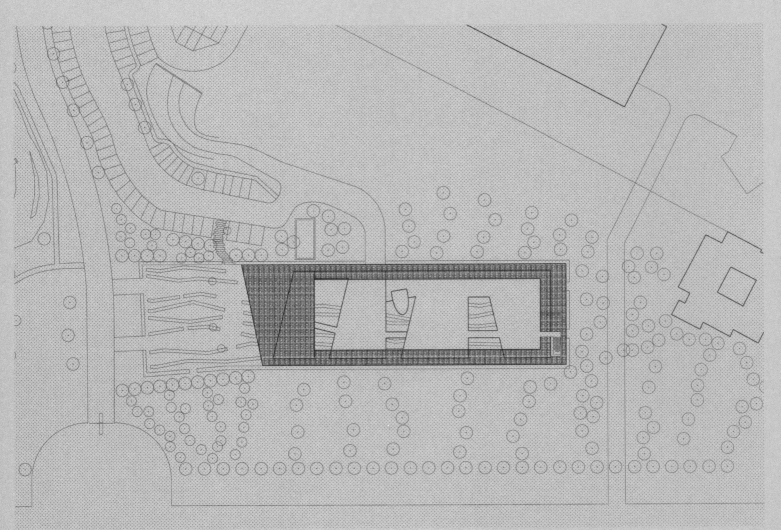

1:1000

E

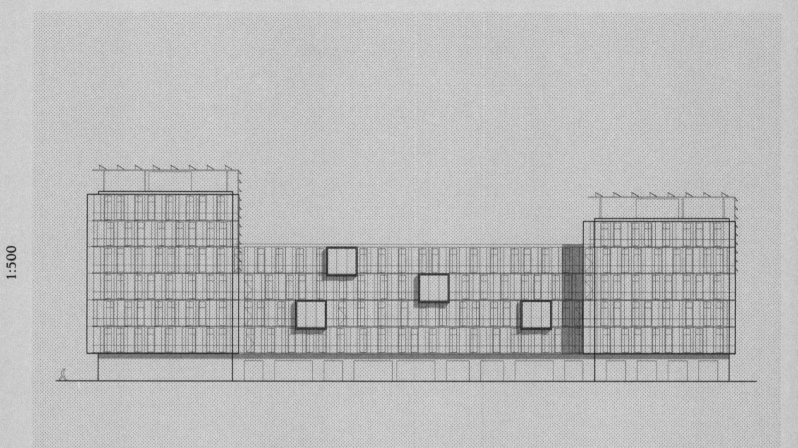

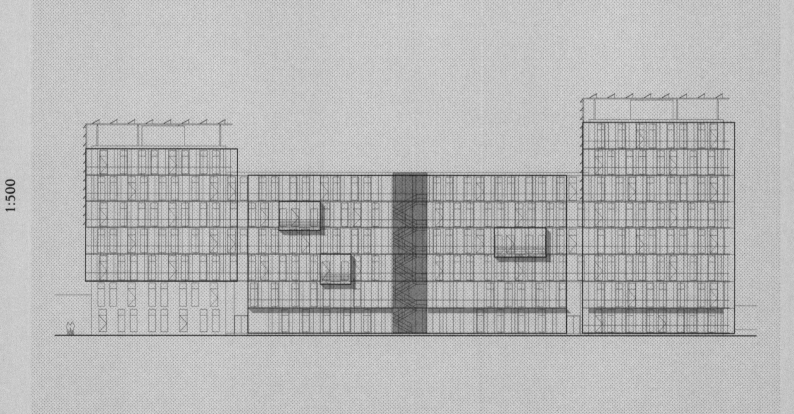

F

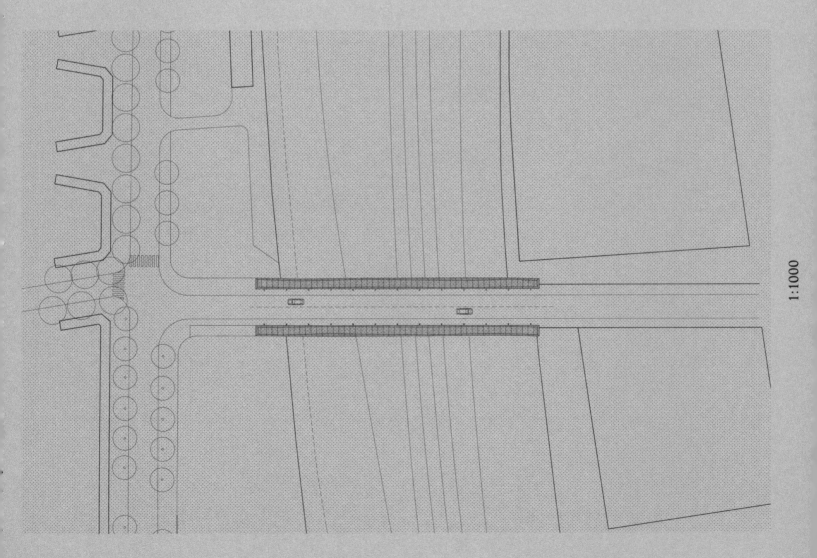

Choisy

G

1:500

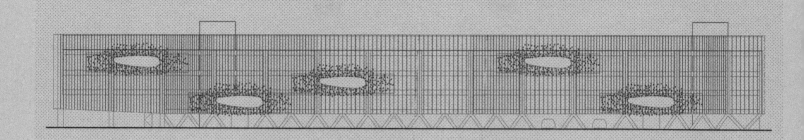

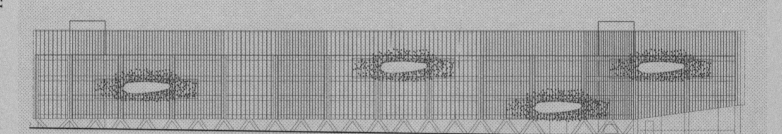

H

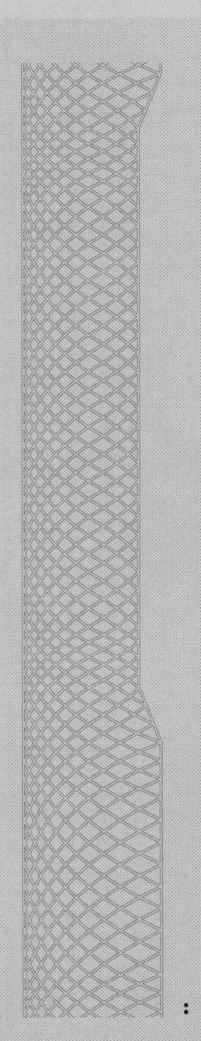

••• 1:1000

•• 1:500

• 1:250

H

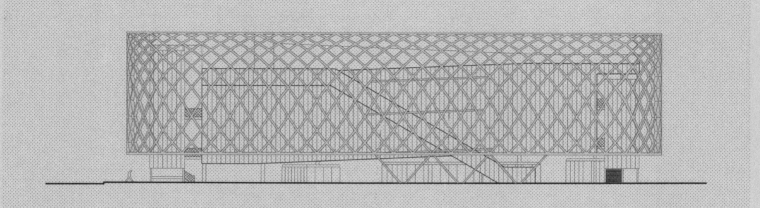

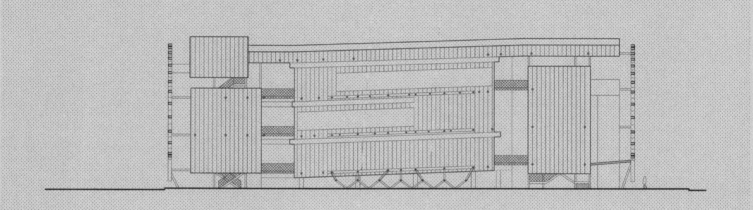

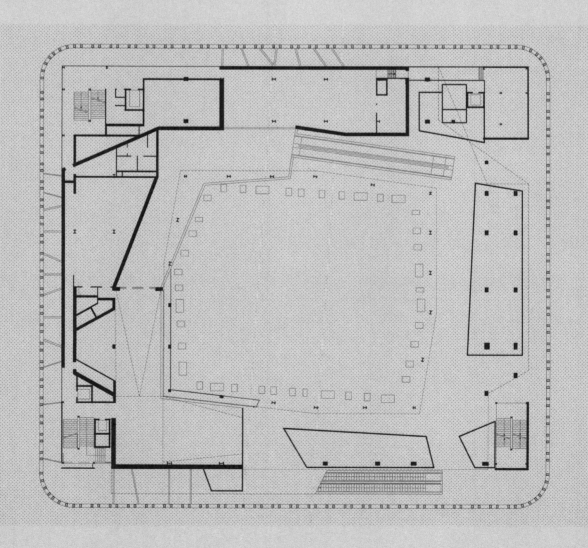

1:500

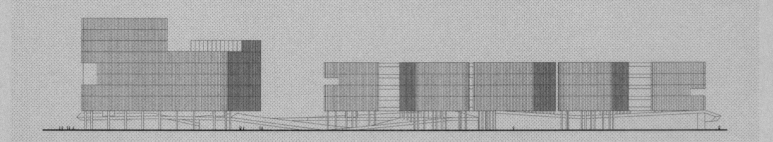

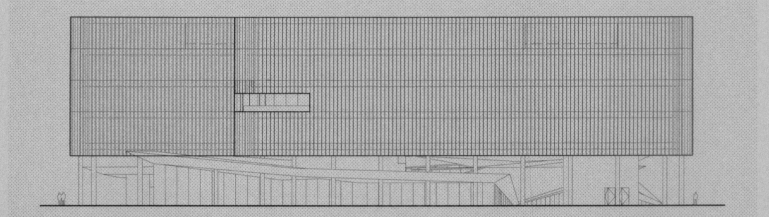

1:2000

1:500

1:1000

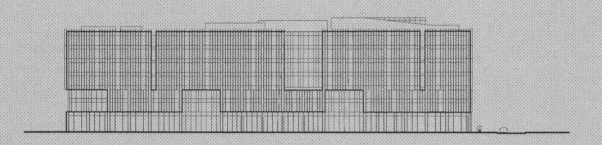

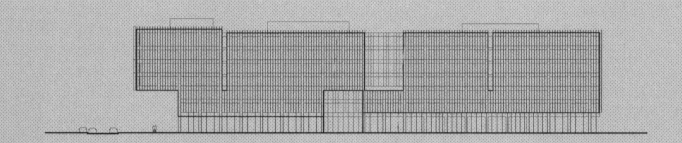

1:500

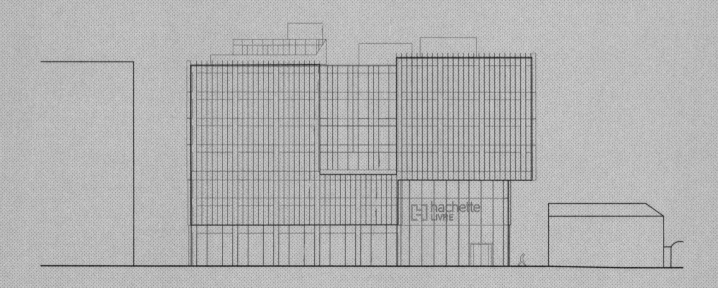

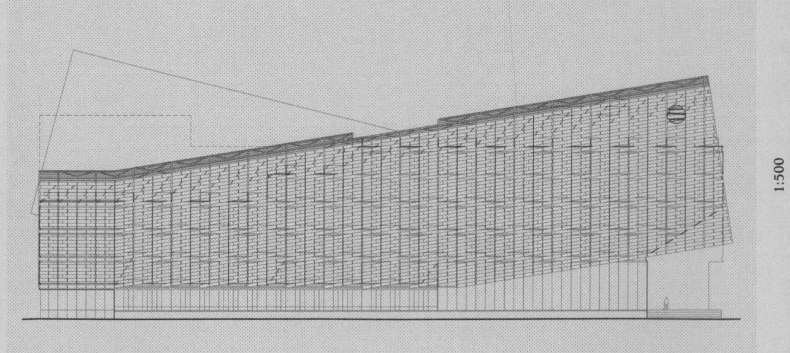

1:500

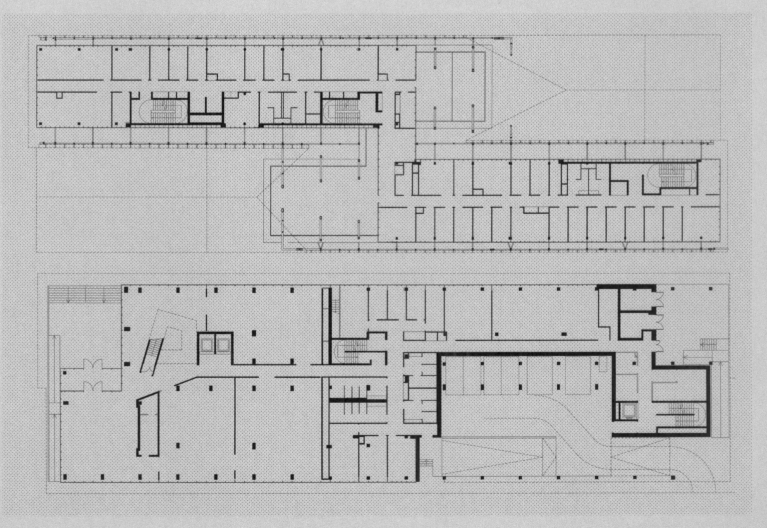

1:500

L

1:500

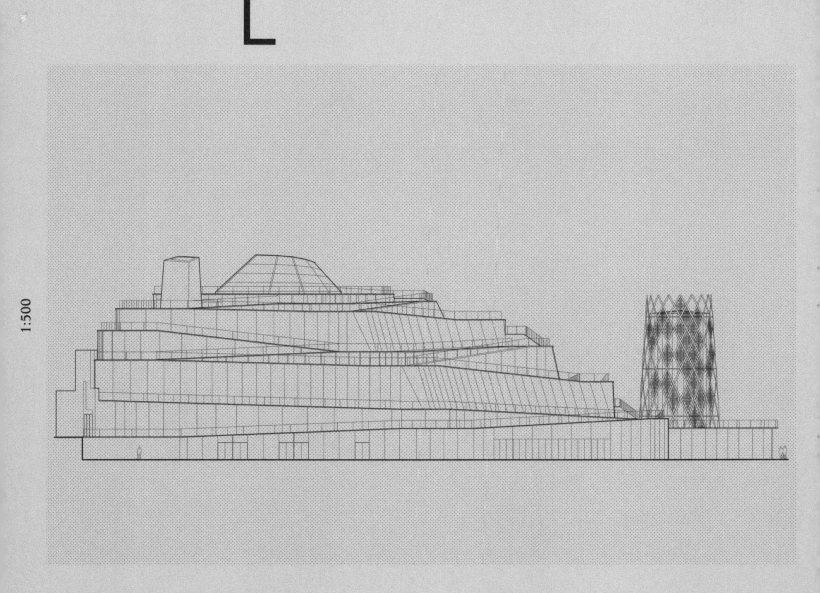

1:500

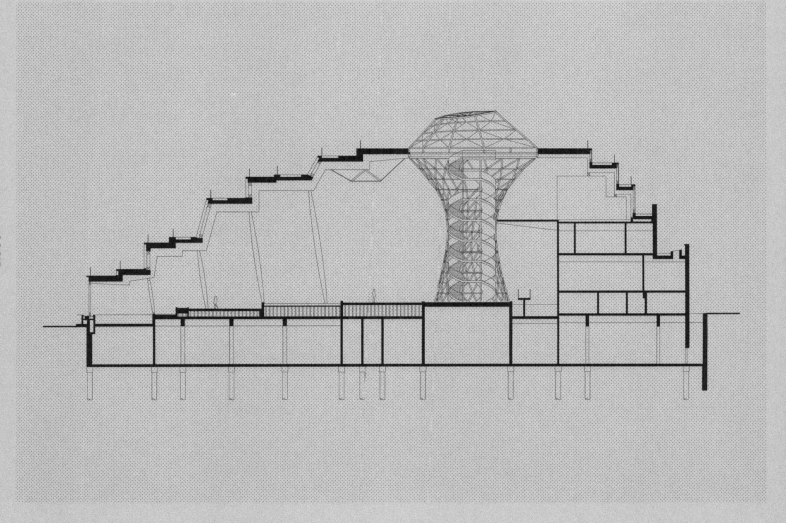

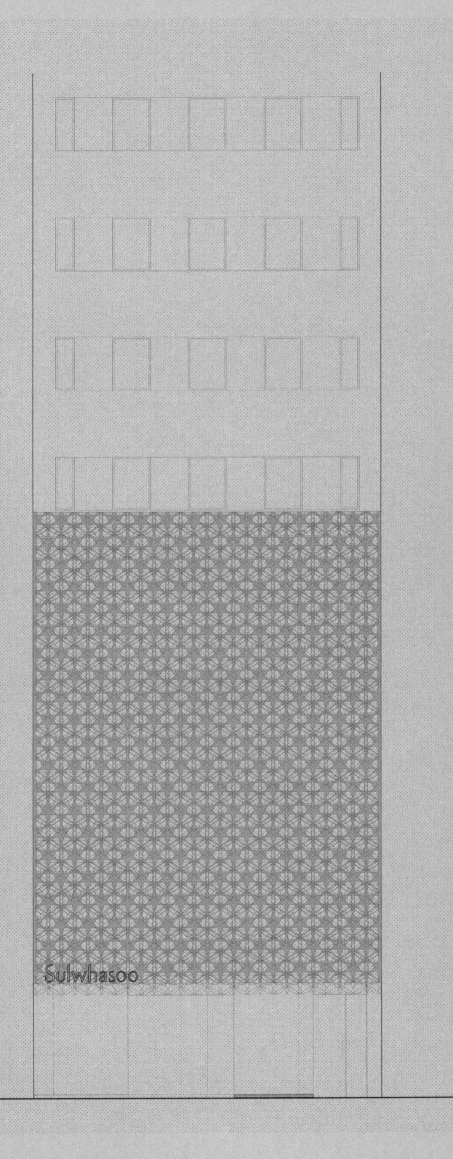

1:100

It is no longer architecture's place to express construction: a provocative statement that reveals a radical shift. The nineteenth century bequeathed to the twentieth the spectacular confusion between expression of structure and architecture of expression. But notions of calculations and materials changed significantly as a result of technological advances and a broadening of the scope of references and disciplines within the architectural field. The skins of buildings, the way elements are interconnected and the incorporation of environmental issues have become just as important as the expression of structure. As Bernard Vaudeville once observed, 'construction has become a liquid phase.'

This trajectory also characterizes Jacques Ferrier's output with respect to the constructed definition of the architectural project. For Ferrier, it is the process of manufacturing and creating, rather than merely building, that is at the heart of his work, at the risk of employing terms more habitually used to talk about an aeroplane, an item of clothing or a car, rather than a building. The construction of the architectural project in his work involves not just the literal resolution of a problem induced by the action of planning and projecting (backing, initiating, covering, making watertight, linking, etc.), but also — and indeed, above all — its resolution within the constraints imposed by strategies of availability. The real difficulty lies in successfully bringing such an operation to fruition: sensing and gauging the very first emotions of the project as the 'manufacturing' process begins, and accepting that any architectural project that is unresolved in terms of this process is an expression of a form of powerlessness. And yet it is precisely this difficulty, at the start of the manufacturing phase, which Ferrier seeks to visualize mentally for each project, through an approach that blends poetry and pragmatism. For him, it is a question not just of sensing and feeling those things revealed by analysis, but also of sensing what the project would feel if it were able to speak.

In this context, Ferrier makes use of his practical and theoretical skills and knowledge, as well as his ability to feel emotions. The principle that guides the development of technical projects in his output could therefore be described in the following terms: at the 'manufacturing' stage, the architectural project must be reconciled with itself and embody the same spirit as when it was nothing but representations, and the spirit of what it will be when it is built. The objective is not to change the architectural project when it enters this stage, but to enrich what is already contained within it. In Ferrier's eyes, a successful project is one that is able to embrace its material limits. With this approach, being 'well built' means living happily with oneself despite the inevitable trials, surprises and restrictions that the manufacturing process necessarily imposes. There are no technical standards capable of responding to and resolving every situation that this process is supposed to represent. The application of a body of standards is an essential accompanying action, but it can never be fully operational once it is brought into contact with the unique nature of a project. The realization of the project is at this point only partial, and it is because Ferrier accepts and acknowledges this fact that he is able to benefit from the freedom this offers.

In architecture, a simple relationship exists between form and construction. Consequently, the choice of building system is a question of the utmost importance. By contrast, the technical aspects (the way in which the chosen construction system is implemented) have little impact on the value of the object. And yet there exists no masterpiece on earth that is not the result of a combination of intelligence and effort. For each project, one must define the rules of composition — in other words, the specific technical constraints that, once taken on board and built upon and adapted, ensure the project is not merely reduced to its practical aspects. In this context, Ferrier questions the ability that technical issues have to define the field of architecture. This is the constructive idea as it might have been defined by Jean Prouvé: the action of mediation by which architecture is brought back to its conditions of production. This mediation is an attempt to draw up a technical narrative that precedes the existence of the object and accompanies its realization.

In a certain way, as Ferrier says himself, it is very much a question of finding and revealing 'the poetry of useful things'.

81

TOUR ISSYGREEN
ISSY LES MOULINEAUX, ZAC CŒUR DE VILLE
BOUYGUES IMMOBILIER
2007_FAISABILITÉ / ESQUISSE

TOUR PORTE DE CLICHY
CLICHY _ ZAC ENTRÉE DE VILLE
BOUYGUES IMMOBILIER
2007_CONCOURS

TOUR GAN
COURBEVOIE, LA DÉFENSE
FONCIÈRE DES RÉGIONS
2007_CONCOURS

TOUR D2
COURBEVOIE, LA DÉFENSE
BOUYGUES IMMOBILIER _ SOGEPROM
2007_CONCOURS

TOUR HERMITAGE
COURBEVOIE, LA DÉFENSE 1
HERMITAGE IMMOBILIER
2007_2008_CONCOURS SIGNAL

AÉROSPACE CAMPUS
TOULOUSE
BOUYGUES IMMOBILIER _ SACRESA
2007_CONCOURS

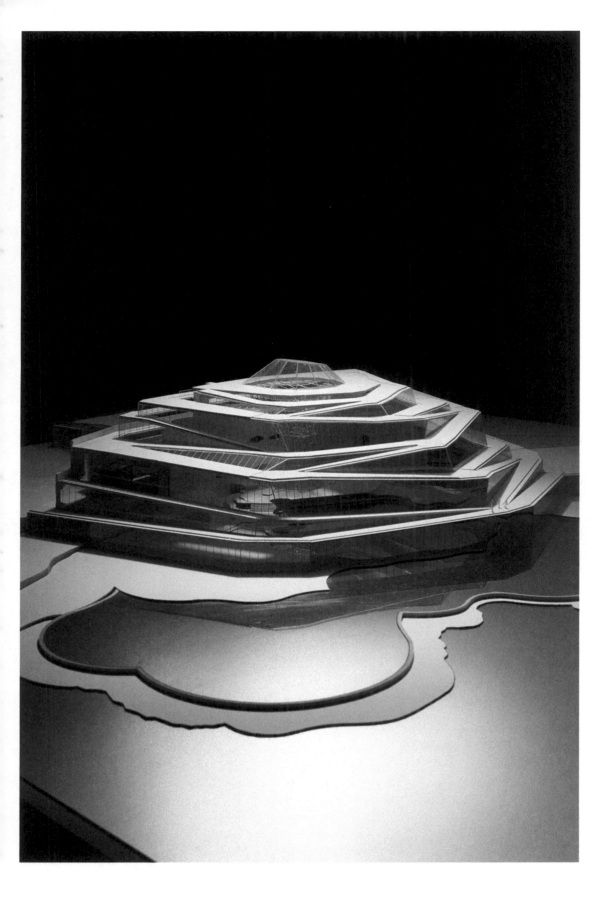

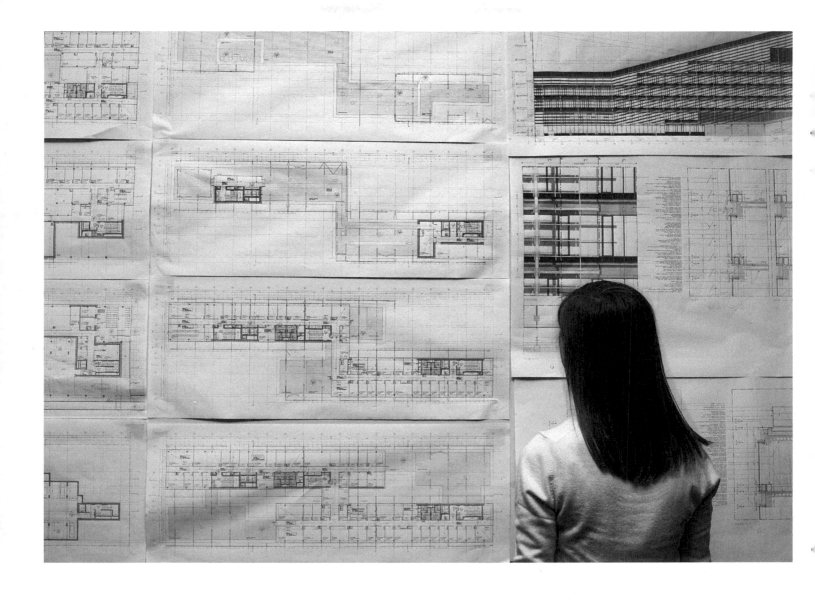

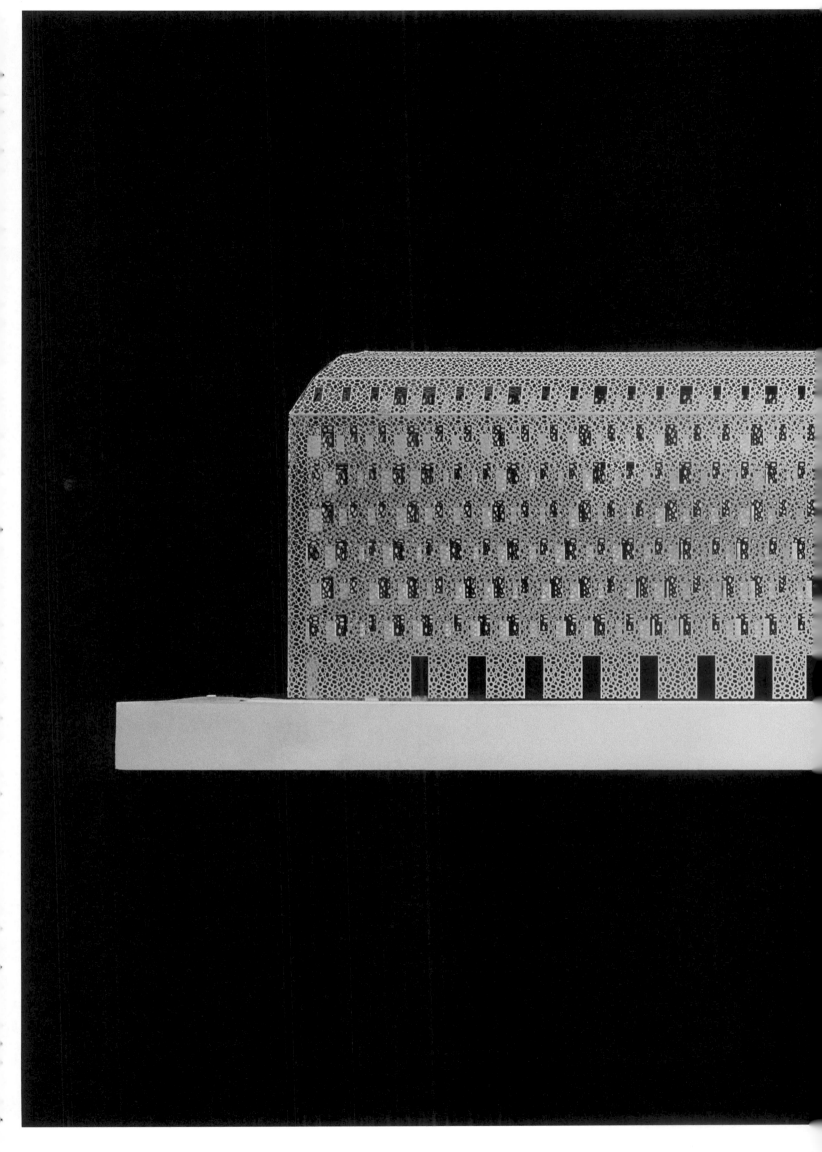

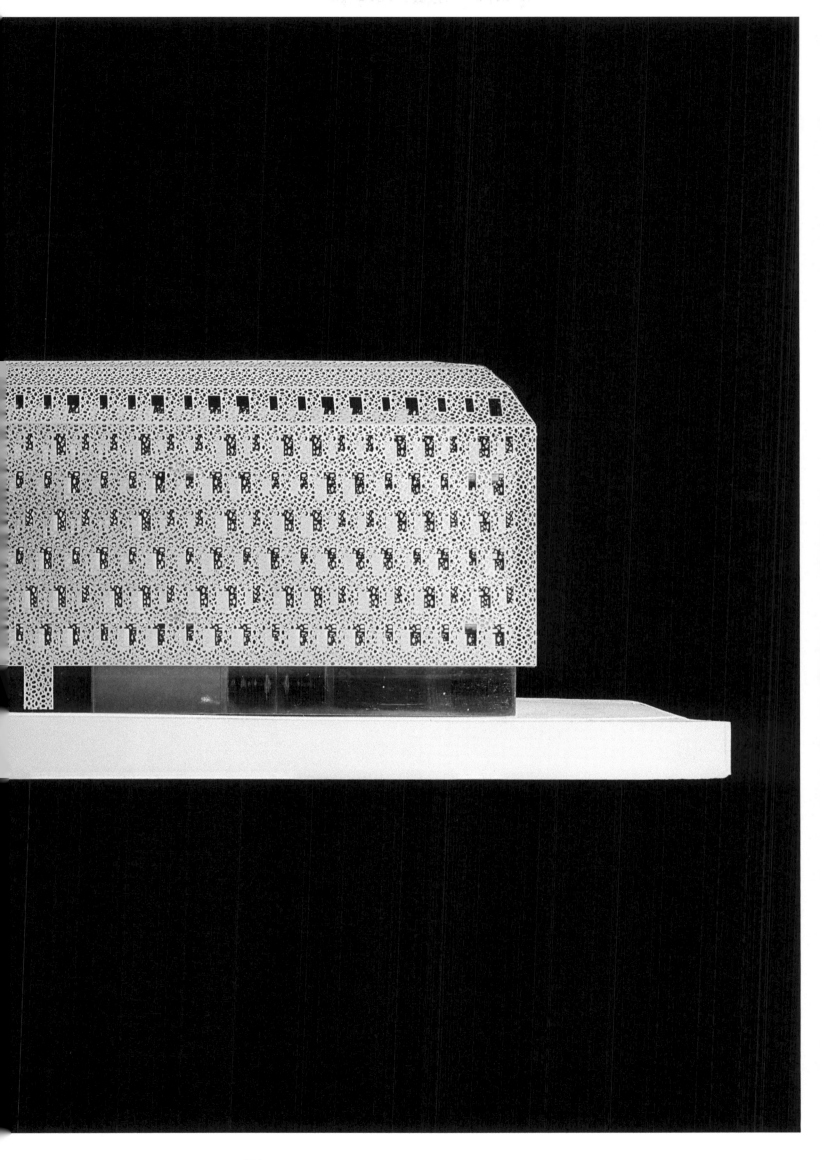

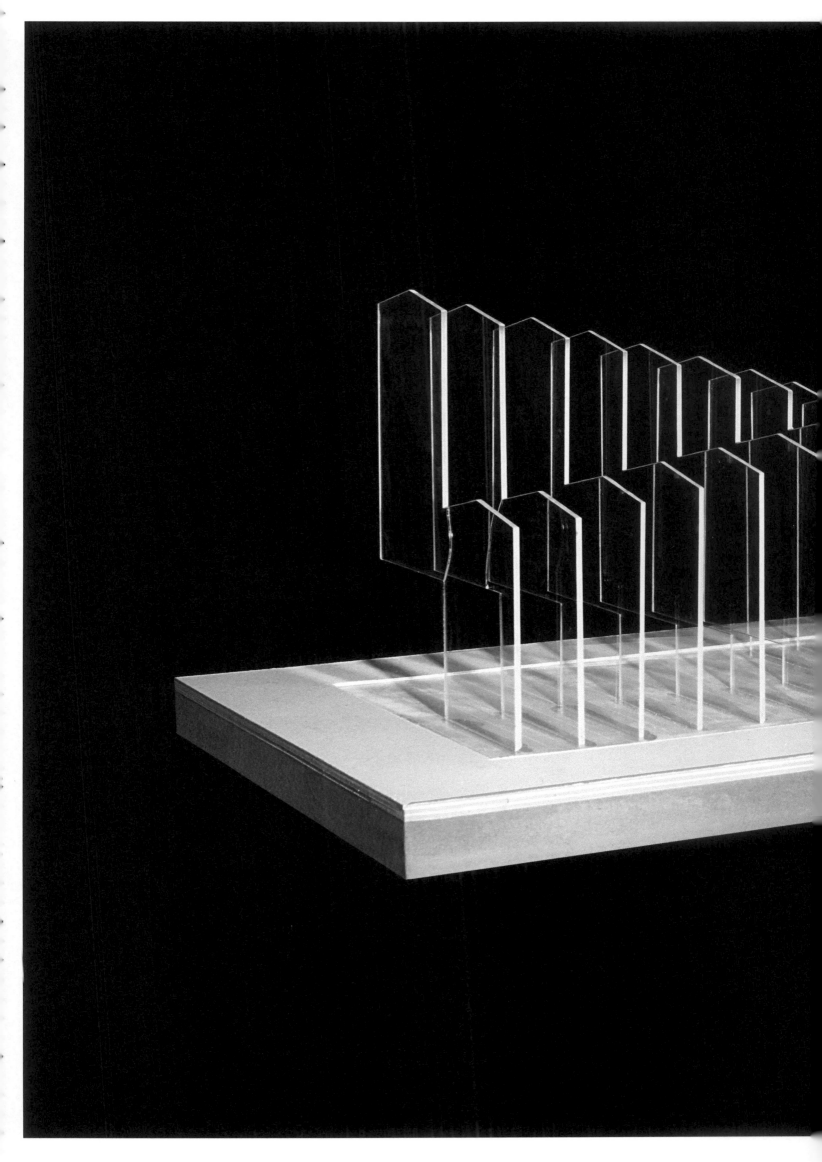

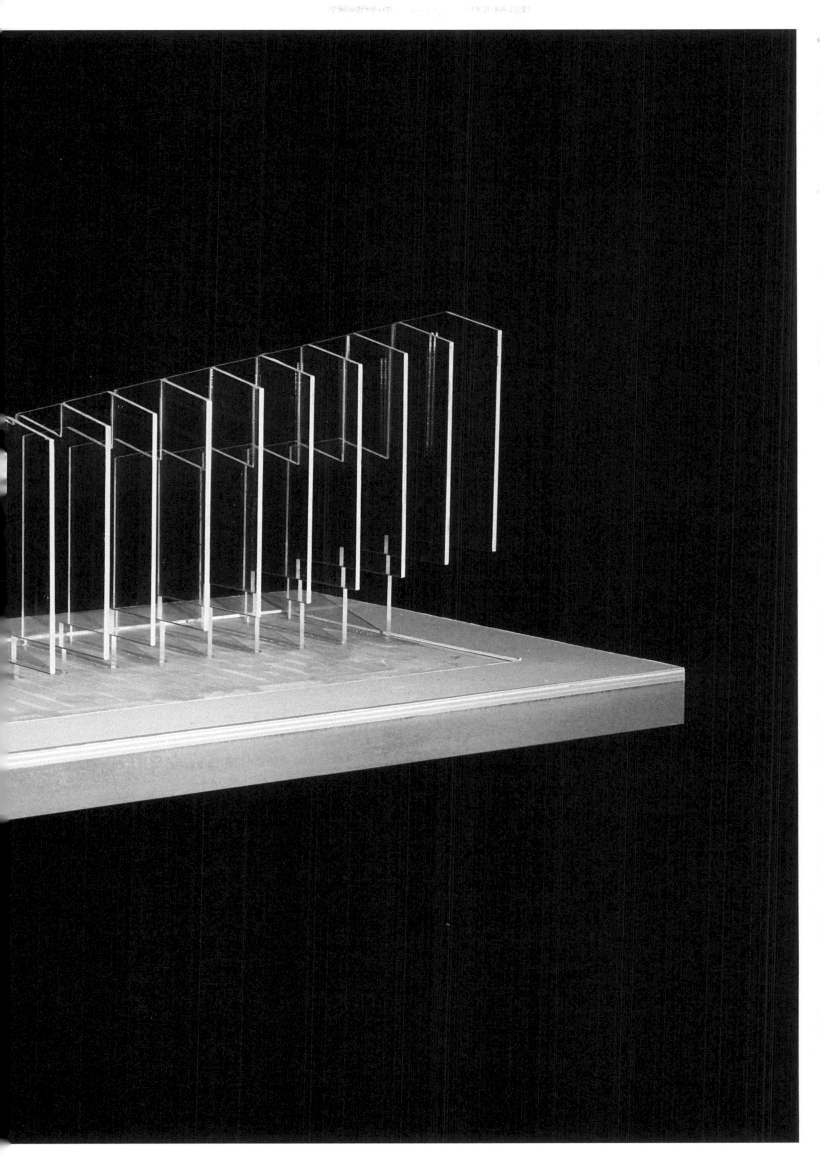

'Curious' (reflecting the title of a journal created by Jacques and others in 1994: <u>Dépliant, pour architectes et autres curieux</u>, or <u>Pamphlet for architects and their curious minds</u>) is perhaps the word that best describes Jacques the architect's first flaw. This curiosity is his means of immersing himself in the 'universe' of his projects. If I were to describe those times when we explore a subject in search of ideas to get a project rolling, there is always a phase of hesitation, of silence even, where we retreat to our respective note pads: his is black and always very organized, as it has been for the last twenty years; mine, by contrast, always full of scribbles noted down any old how, so messy that a graphologist would surely say that I was not rigorous enough to be an architect.

Ah, rigour, there's another of Jacques' flaws: his passion for round numbers, sequences, proportions and applied mathematics in general, which he uses to resolve functional problems with ease. I'm lost as soon he starts doing his calculations to ensure that the drawings will withstand whatever unforeseen circumstances may crop up during the project's development. To start with, there's always an addition, followed by a multiplication, then a subtraction from that total and then… Jacques falls silent and continues his exercise. Sometimes he irritates me when he says to me at the end, 'You see?' or 'You agree, yes?'

How does he expect me to be in agreement when I can't even follow his reasoning? As for reason, I wouldn't say it was a flaw of his, exactly. Rather, I would say he knows how to sidestep it – and thank goodness, he does! It might seem contradictory that what appears to be a highly Cartesian mind also allows him to imagine buildings that are so sensual and poetic. That said (and here's the paradox) he does not belong to that category of illogical architects who shut themselves away in their imagination. Imaginative is something Jacques has to be when he is designing and then constantly reworking a project, adapting it in conjunction with the many other people who gravitate around him. I wish I could describe these scenes when, while seeking a solution or approval or sometimes even permission, he puts his vast and varied general knowledge to use in order to find arguments to support his ideas. Moreover, it is his references from outside the field of architecture that are typically the most incisive. He has this ability to federate opinion and foster support, which is just as well when it comes to, for example, changing the colour of a façade on a project site, the kind of situation that calls for persuasion in spades!

And if there's one thing Jacques is, it's persuasive, thanks to his boundless natural charisma. I've not seen many people get the better of him. He often gets what he wants, sometimes, it has to be said, as a result of the air of innocent bewilderment he adopts when he wishes to give the impression of not having understood the difficulty or criticism in question. When that happens, I know he'll end up getting his way. People often say he has a dazzling mind. Being dazzling in society isn't his thing, though. He can even be a little untamed in this respect, choosing his friends in the same way as he chooses his projects. When asked who inspires him, he readily cites the illusionist and film-maker Georges Méliès for his ability to create magic out of very simple things, an inspiration attested to by the new offices for Piper-Heidsieck in Reims D. I visited the site on a sunny day (it was the start of my collaboration with Jacques, long before we became associates), and I remember feeling a great deal of emotion as I fully appreciated the richness of the seemingly simple façade that he had created.

p. 137

And he has certainly been enriched by choosing to remain a free-thinking architect defending a certain vision of the profession, one that he exercises with emotion but without excess – another major flaw that goes completely against the spirit of the times, which prefers 'starchitects' to humanistic architecture. I look forward to the day when, weary of short-term special effects, the public comes to its senses and yearns once again for something more meaningful. When that day arrives, Jacques the humanist architect will be above the stars on cloud nine.

A

A

B

C

E

E

F

F

172

Bienvenue dans le Pavillon France

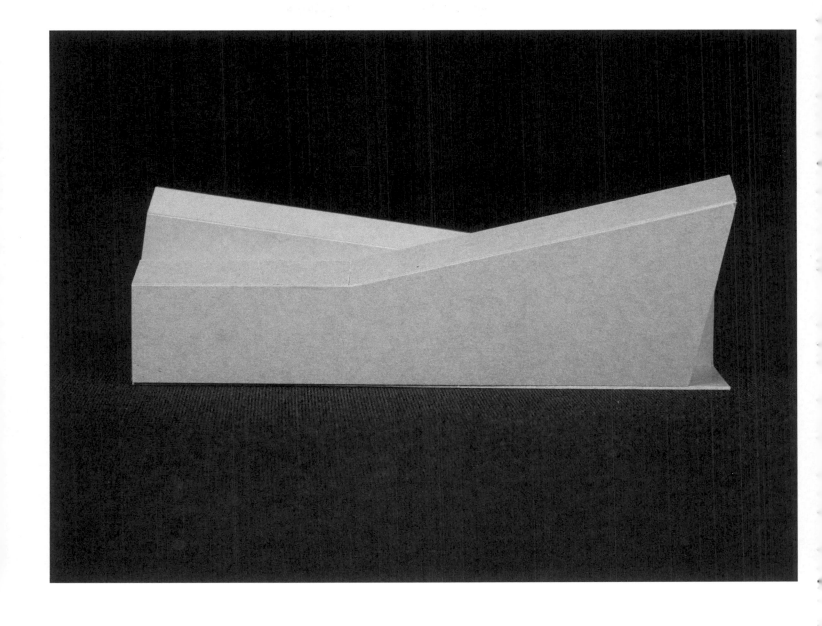

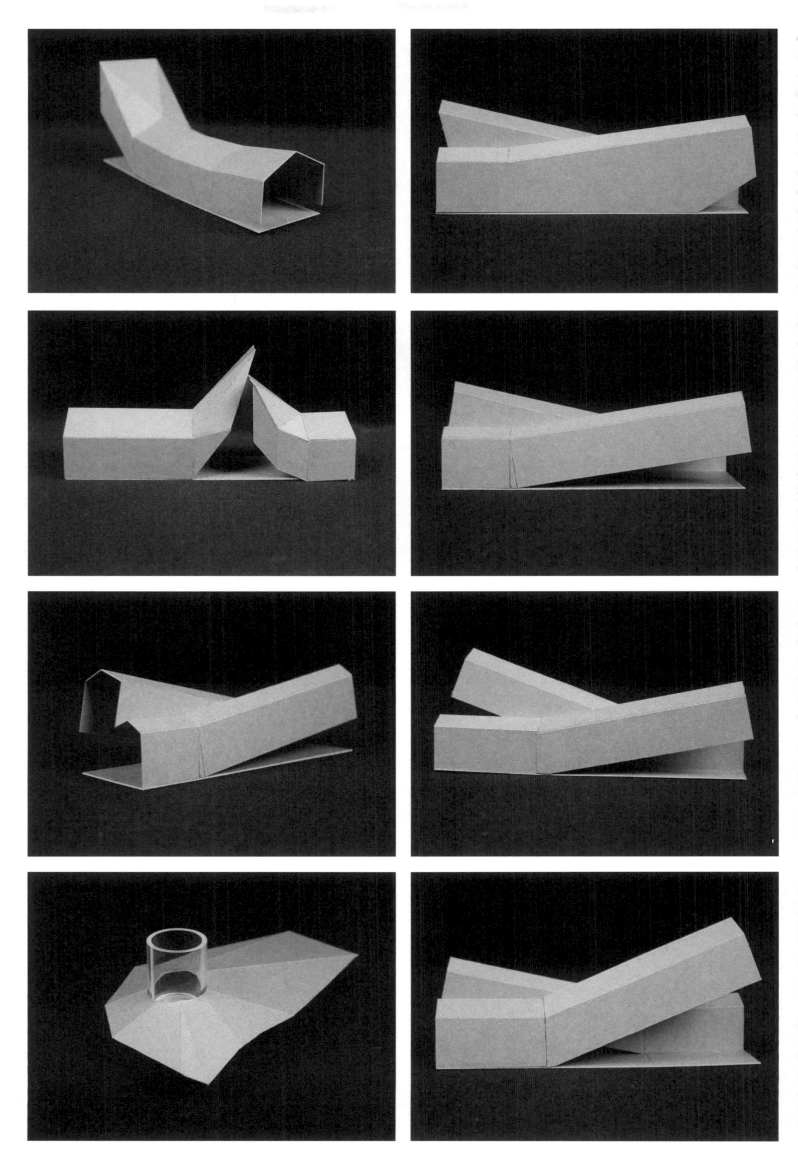

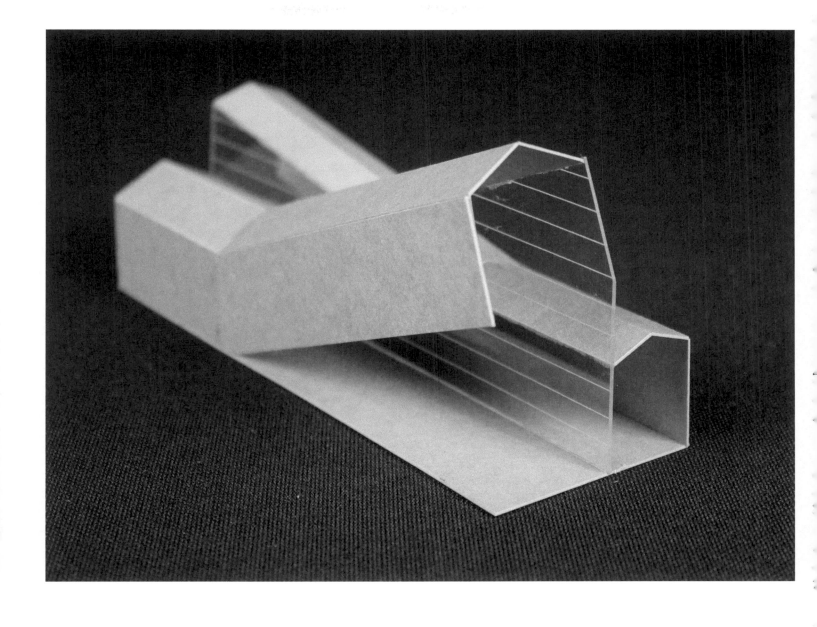

L

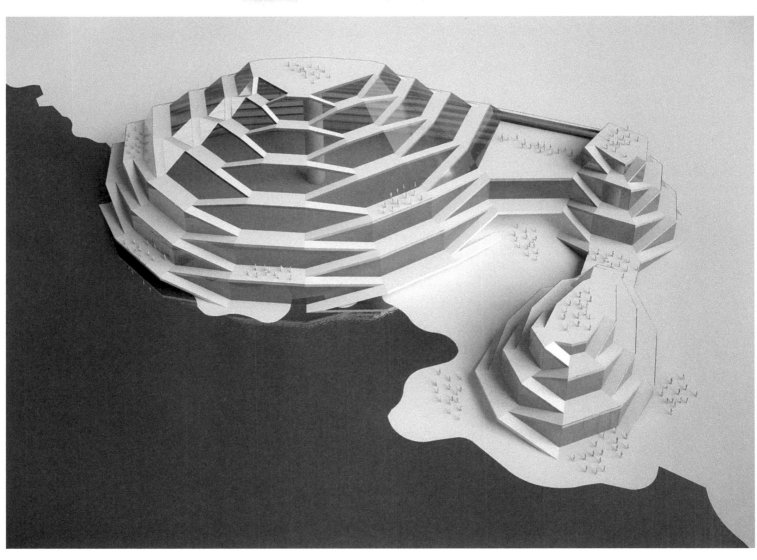

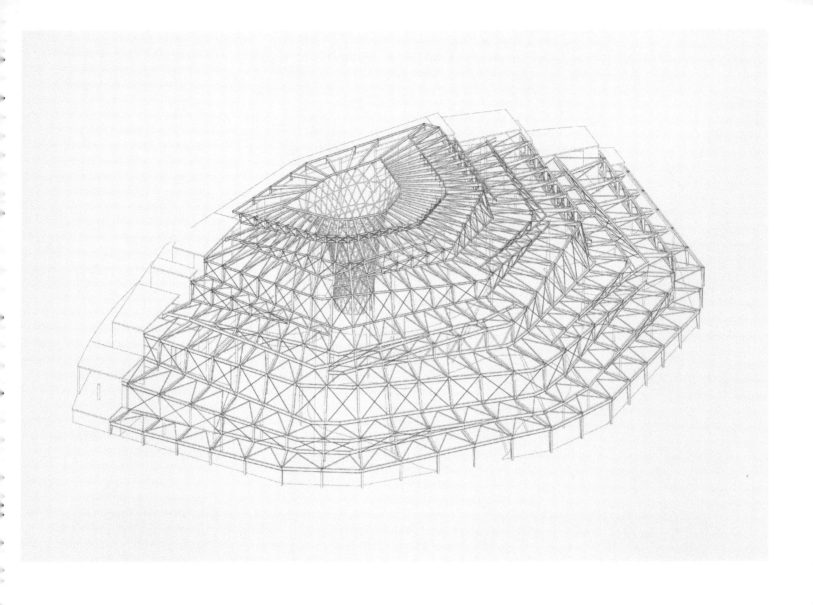

L

	A	**B**	**C**
City	Bordeaux	Lorient	Toulouse
Country	(FR)	(FR)	(FR)
Project	Tramway Maintenance Depot	Éric-Tabarly Sailing Museum	Airbus Delivery Centre
Year	2003	2007	2006

A

This project was one result of the dramatic reinvention of Bordeaux for the twenty-first century. New buildings and the regeneration of historic areas were key elements of this campaign of renewal, but hardly less significant has been the development of a new transport system based on the reintroduction of trams: three lines, with a total extent of 44 km (27 miles), opened between 2003–8, with further extensions planned. The practice was commissioned to design the principal maintenance depot for the tramway system, located on a site close to the Garonne river, at the edge of the Bastide district. The project is part of a regeneration programme for this previously rundown quarter, across the river from the city centre. In essence, the depot is an industrial shed in the best functional tradition of the nineteenth century, reflecting Ferrier's respect for the great engineers of the time. A linear progression of three linked buildings contains workshops, a maintenance centre and storage shed for the tram units. A single structural system encloses the entire depot, providing column-free internal spaces. It combines rationality with expressive drama and is highly economical. Great copper-clad waves, spanning 22 m (72 ft) each and supported on 30 m (98 ft)-span gantries, incorporate strips of glazing that channel controlled natural light into the working spaces. External walls contain large areas of translucent glazing that glow after dark with opaque views into the depot.

B

Named in honour of the famous Breton yachtsman Éric Tabarly (1931–98), the museum occupies a site on the waterfront at Lorient, in Brittany. Nearby is a grim but impressive reminder of the maritime city's history: the German U-boat depot, a massive concrete structure that allied bombers failed to destroy during the Second World War, and is now a tourist attraction. Ferrier's building, lightweight and open, provides a deliberate contrast to the monumentality of this wartime relic. The museum houses permanent and temporary exhibition spaces (Tabarly's yacht, Pen Duick V, is a prized exhibit), with a cinema, restaurant and more, and is an important element in the regeneration of the city's former docklands. The building is south-facing and opens up to fine views of the ocean. Its plan is simple and immediately legible: a contemporary reinterpretation of the traditional maritime shed. Indeed, the structure's functional elegance draws on the local tradition of boat and ship-building, with its landmark tower evoking a great mast as it extends into the water. The curvaceous form is equally reminiscent of the hull of some great ocean-going vessel. Extensive areas of solar panels form part of the low-energy servicing agenda.

C

The city of Toulouse is the home of Airbus, an international aircraft manufacturer that employs more than 60,000 people in France, the UK, Germany and Spain. Ferrier's delivery centre, formally opened in 2007 by President Nicolas Sarkozy and the German chancellor Angela Merkel, is both highly functional and a showcase for the company's designs (an Airbus 380 costs around ten times as much as the delivery centre did to build). The 18,500 m² (199,132 sq ft) building incorporates a gallery with a curved glazed façade, where VIPs and press can view the aircraft. A huge reception area, the spectacular Sky Hall, includes a restaurant, bar and auditorium, under a glazed roof shaded by solar panels. A covered balcony extends along the entire length of the façade, and provision has been made for visitors who wish to arrive by private jet, rather than using the adjacent airport. Full security and customs facilities reinforce the feeling of the building as an airport terminal. A monumental canopy on the southern side provides shelter for visitors arriving by car. Three levels of offices are arranged around two internal courts, and four circular satellite buildings, connected to the centre, contain accommodation for maintenance teams at ground level. Above is a level that serves as a base for clients while taking delivery of aircraft. This is a building designed to impress, but with a clear and practical agenda.

	A	**B**	**C**
Plans	65	66	67
Photographs	101–12	113–22	123–34

	D	E	F
City	Reims	Grenoble	Choisy
Country	(FR)	(FR)	(FR)
Project	Piper-Heidsieck Offices	Office Development	Bridge
Year	2008	2009	2010

The champagne firm Piper-Heidsieck can trace its origins back to 1785. But despite its venerable history, the company is a dynamic, international business that is continually looking to the future. This ethos is reflected in its decision to quit its historic base in the centre of Reims and relocate its production and administration arms some distance out of the city, to a developing business district close to the Champagne-Ardenne TGV station (a forty-minute journey from Gare de l'Est). Working closely with the firm's CEO, who had a clear agenda for the new complex, Ferrier developed designs for a highly practical office building that was also memorable, with a clear element of symbolism. Given the traditional conservatism of the champagne industry, the commission was a bold move. The essence of the project lies in the series of four linked steel-framed pavilions, with a total of 2,000 m² (21,528 sq ft) of accommodation across two storeys for around sixty staff, contained within an external metal skin. The building is immediately adjacent to the production facility, which produces around 6 million bottles of champagne a year, both sharing a carefully conceived landscape. The office pavilions have a minimalist elegance achieved by careful detailing: only the entrance lobby contains references to the wine trade. The external skin features four distinct panel patterns of laser-cut aluminium, which extend outwards to form an impressive entrance canopy. A gold coating evokes the colour of champagne and, on a fine day, lends the building's skin something of champagne's effervescent character.

The requirements of this project meant working within the constraints of an existing masterplan to a programme and budget set by a speculative developer. Ferrier's brief was to design the external envelope of the 12,000 m² (129,167 sq ft) building with no involvement in its exterior massing, which was already established, or the interior. The municipal authorities wanted a distinctive structure on the site, which is close to the Autoroute de Suisse and clearly visible from the banks of the Drac river, with a backdrop of alpine peaks. The double-skin on three elevations, with an external layer composed of gold aluminium panels, provides a highly effective sunscreen for the office spaces, with openings arranged to provide views from each office and supply diffused light inside. Amenities for the office workers include accessible terraces and glazed loggias with mountain views on the western façade. The design for the building envelope embodies a number of devices that contribute to a sustainable environmental agenda, with solar panels supplying 25 per cent of energy needs. The double-skin provides a high level of insulation, the success of which has led to other commissions for office buildings requiring the same high level of environmental performance. The project exemplifies the practice's expertise in transforming superficially ordinary buildings both aesthetically and in terms of environmental performance and user benefits.

Ferrier's design for a bridge at Choisy, in the southeastern suburbs of Paris, is part of a regeneration strategy for an isolated former industrial area between the Seine, where there was a heavy concentration of wharves, and busy railway tracks. Bridging the tracks opened up the area to new development. The 70 m (230 ft)-long bridge, which provides for two lanes of traffic with footpaths on either side, had to provide a clear span, with no intermediate supports. There also could not be any interruption to train services during the construction period. The main beams carrying the structure were pre-assembled on site and then lifted into place. What is distinctive about the bridge is the cladding of perforated aluminium wrapped around the structure, a classic device of the architect's that is in tune with his desire to create more enjoyable public places. He cites Christo and Jeanne-Claude's famous 'wrapping' of the Pont Neuf in 1985 as one of his inspirations. The bridge appears to most striking effect after dark, when a ghostly green light gives it an ethereal presence in the townscape. The project is a striking example of the way that lighting technology can add a new dimension to architecture.

	G	H	I
City	Soissons	Shanghai	Shanghai
Country	(FR)	(CH)	(CH)
Project	Multi-storey Car Park	French Pavilion	Yidian Office Building
Year	2009	2010	2014

This project exemplifies Ferrier's ability to transform an ordinary structure into something memorable and enjoyable through economical means. The 600-space car park, in the shadow of the medieval church of St-Jean-des-Vignes, is part of the ongoing redevelopment of a former military base into a new business quarter for the city of Soissons, in northern France. Parking is provided over five staggered levels. The concrete structure is relatively conventional, with large, open floor spans that have minimal interventions and screens of galvanized steel mesh at the perimeter. It is overlaid with an external skin of weathered timber, set forward in line with fire regulations. Varying the rhythm and angle of the timber slats achieves the effect of depth and movement, and at each level, an eye-shaped opening with views over the city provides space for planting, reminiscent of hanging gardens. Ferrier addressed the issue of navigation by using large photographic images at each half-level, inspired by the memory game devised by Charles and Ray Eames. The device is playful yet highly practical. What could have been a purely functional structure has become a memorable addition to the changing townscape.

Winning the competition to design the French Pavilion for the Shanghai Expo 2010 was a major coup for the practice, but it was also significant in the development of ideas that would eventually lead to the establishment of the Sensual City Studio in 2011. A notable feature of the commission was that Ferrier was in charge of both the architecture and the fit-out of the pavilion, which was conceived as a multi-sensory experience. The display area, restaurant and other spaces were arranged around a central courtyard with gardens designed by Michel Hoessler that extend onto the roof of the building. The pavilion is a highly flexible container, clad in plastic panels, with an external skin of steel coated in glass fibre-reinforced concrete. The cross-braced mesh cladding was part of a design strategy intended to create the effect of a structure floating on a pool of water. The structural rationale was to allow the internal spaces to be column-free. Visitors were conveyed to the top of the building by means of a double escalator and a gently sloping ramp suspended over the water pool. They were introduced first to the gardens, and then to the interior of the pavilion, forming a continuous experience. The pavilion proved to be so popular, with up to 100,000 visitors daily, that, uniquely among the national pavilions, it was retained after the Expo and converted into a contemporary art museum.

Following the success of the French Pavilion, Ferrier was commissioned to design this substantial office complex for a site sandwiched between a main road and one of Shanghai's canals. The project stands apart from many recent developments in the city for its commitment to the idea of a 'built landscape', which fuses architecture and nature to create a more liveable urban environment. Its provision of generous open space along the banks of the canal gives the city a precious 'lung'. The masterplan for the site breaks down the office accommodation into a series of blocks of up to ten storeys, mostly orientated north-south, a coherent grouping but with a variety of forms created by folds and cut-backs to their façades, which reduces the perceived scale and creates a variety of vistas through the development. The ground level of the buildings was conceived as an extension of the surrounding landscape, a lively place for a mix of uses, including provision for small businesses, which in turn form a natural extension of the city. The façades of the buildings are equipped with a series of vertical blades that baffle the sunlight: one side of the blades is ceramic-coated, coloured green or blue; the other left as polished aluminium, so that the perception of the buildings is constantly changing, depending on the viewpoint. The project represents a serious attempt to inject a new sensuality into Shanghai within the constraints of a commercial brief.

Plans	71	72-3	74
Photographs	167-78	179-94	195-204

	J	K	L
City	Vanves	Rouen	Paris
Country	(FR)	(FR)	(FR)
Project	Hachette Headquarters	Métropole Rouen Normandie	Aqualagon
Year	2015	2017	2016

The decision by the publishing company Hachette to move its headquarters from central Paris to Vanves, beyond the Périphérique, was a radical one, which is reflected in this highly innovative building. The project, a winning competition entry from 2010, had to address the challenge of a constricted site in a densely built-up urban area contained on one side by a busy railway line. The mixed nature of the adjacent development, with modest nineteenth-century residences contrasting with bulky office and apartment buildings, was a further challenge in terms of determining an appropriate scale for the new building. The obvious location for the main entrance was at the northwestern corner of the site. The western façade of the building is set back from the site boundary to create a generous landscaped space, the papyrus garden, which forms a green oasis in the city. In the summer months, the garden acts as an extension to the ground floor, where the reception area, with its array of bookcases displaying some of the company's products, staff restaurant, boardroom and meeting rooms form a progression of spaces. The offices are designed for collaborative working, with flexible spaces accommodating the various publishing imprints within the Hachette empire. The aim was to allow each of these operations to put its own stamp on its working space. The controlled use of natural light, via an outer skin of slatted blinds, is part of a low-energy environmental agenda.

This project is the winning entry from a 2013 competition for the headquarters of Métropole Rouen Normandie, a regional authority covering a wide area around the city of Rouen. The site for the building is across the Seine from the heart of the old city in a former industrial area, now the focus of a major regeneration campaign. A building with qualities that reflect the agenda of renewal, therefore, was an essential part of the brief. Ferrier provided this, but also infused the building with subtle reminders of the area's industrial past. A further requirement was that the building must have exemplary eco-credentials; the aim was nothing less than a zero-energy strategy. The project combines practicality and economy of means with an element of delight. Monet painted some of his most memorable canvases in Rouen, and Ferrier's use of refracting glass and colour on the building's façade evokes the Impressionists' use of natural light through the creation of a constantly changing series of reflections. Solar panels form a key part of the environmental agenda of the building, which has been conceived as a symbol of regional revival.

Disneyland Paris, located in Marne-la-Vallée, 30 km (19 miles) east of the capital, is one of Europe's largest visitor attractions. This winning competition entry is part of the larger Villages Nature scheme, a collaboration between Disney and Center Parcs, and forms a natural complement to Disneyland. Three 'villages' of tourist accommodation are planned around a new lake and woodlands. Ferrier's building forms the centrepiece of the development and is, in the great tradition of Buckminster Fuller's geodesic domes, an envelope for an artificial climate. The project is driven by a progressive environmental agenda, with nearly all the heating requirements provided by geothermal technology. In response to a demanding brief, the building has been designed for enjoyment. It is conceived as a spiral, with an economical structure providing a sensational promenade that takes visitors through densely planted gardens, which will provide a habitat for a variety of animals. The skin of the building is as minimal as that of a circus tent; it is formed of timber with steel connectors, but has an ethereal element of transparency. Columns are made of an ultra-high performance fibre-reinforced concrete. This combination of structural integrity and connection to the natural world reflects the same thinking that drove the French Pavilion. The project is a striking new interpretation of the great glasshouses of the nineteenth century, re-imagined for the leisure industry of today.

Plans	75	76	77
Photographs	205–18	219–28	229–46

Jacques Ferrier is an architect and urban planner. Following his architectural training at the École Nationale Supérieure d'Architecture de Paris-Belleville and the École Centrale Paris, he set up his own architectural firm in 1993, in Paris, and has worked both in France and on the international stage. The agency's output is all based on the same philosophy: the creation of an architecture and cities that contribute to a sustainable society. His humanistic vision for tomorrow's cities is most fully expressed in the concept of the Sensual City, which seeks to answer the question of what urban design and planning should be today.

Alexander Tzonis was educated at Yale University and taught at Harvard 1967–81. He is Professor Emeritus at the Delft University of Technology and visiting professor at Tsinghua University, in Beijing. Through his numerous books, research projects and lecturing across the globe, he has brought together scientific and humanistic approaches in a rare synthesis. He has written extensively on the work of Jacques Ferrier.

Kenneth Powell is an architecture critic and journalist based in London. He contributes to newspapers and journals in both the UK and abroad and is a former architecture correspondent for the Daily Telegraph. Powell's many books include monographs on Norman Foster and Will Alsop, as well as a three-volume study on the work of Richard Rogers. He was elected Honorary Fellow of the Royal Institute of British Architects in 2000.

Jean-Marc Weill is an architect and engineer, and graduate of the École Nationale Supérieure d'Architecture de Nancy, Harvard and the Conservatoire National des Arts et Métiers, Paris. He has collaborated with Jacques Ferrier on many projects, including the French Pavilion at the Shanghai World Expo 2010, the Airbus Delivery Centre and Aqualagon. Weill also teaches at various universities and is chairman of C & E Ingénierie in Paris.

Pauline Marchetti is a state-registered architect, and graduated from the École Nationale Supérieure d'Architecture de Paris-Belleville. She led the French Pavilion project for Shanghai Expo 2010, and in the same year founded the Sensual City Studio with Jacques Ferrier, in partnership with Philippe Simay. Under her leadership, the studio focuses on developing an innovative and alternative approach for a humanistic urban design.

The work of Jacques Ferrier has been featured widely in the international architectural press. For more information, please visit www.jacques-ferrier.com, where a full and regularly updated bibliography can be found.

A+U
AIT Best of Europe
AMC
Arca International
Archiscopie
Archistorm
Architectura Construcao
Architectural Record
Architectures à Vivre
Architecture d'aujourd'hui
Arquitectura y Diseno
Arquitectura & Urbanismo
AV Proyectos
Bauwelt
Beaux-Arts
Bob
Building
Bund
Cahiers Techniques du bâtiment
Ça m'intéresse
Capital
China News
Chine Plus
Citizen K
Competition
Connaissance des Arts
Construire
Côté Ouest
Côté Sud
Crash
Crescendo
Culture et Communication
D'A
Déco
Détails
Ecologik
Elle
Europa
Exé
Frame
Harvard Design Magazine
Herald International Tribune
Homes
IDEAT
Indian Architect & Builder
Interior architecture of China
Intramuros

La Tribune
La Tribune de Bruxelles
Le Figaro
Le Journal du dimanche
Le Monde
Le Moniteur
Le Nouvel Observateur
Le Point
Les Echos
L'Express
Libération
Maison Magazine
Marianne
Marie Claire Maison
New Landscape International
Paris Match
Pasajes Construcción
Perspective
Place Publique
Playboy
Property UE
Quebec Sciences
Résidences Décorations
Revue Urbanisme
Scape
Sciences et avenir
Sciences et vie
Shanghai Daily
Télérama
Time + Architecture
Time
Upstreet
Urban China
Urban Space Design
Usine Nouvelle
Valeurs Actuelles
VSD
Wettbewerbe Aktuell
Winter Property
Zurban

Project credits

All of the projects in this book are the work of Jacques Ferrier Architecture, except for the following:
- École Nationale Supérieure des Mines de Paris, Évry (project no. 1): Jacques Ferrier and François Gruson
- Sagep Water Treatment Plant, Joinville-le-Pont (project no. 2): Jacques Ferrier and François Gruson
- Home of Humanities/Marcel-Saupin, Nantes (project no. 10): FGP/Jacques Ferrier, Philippe Gazeau and Louis Paillard
- Mantilla Ilôt, Montpellier (project no. 11): Jacques Ferrier Architecture/A+ Architecture
- Odysseum station, Montpellier (project no. 12): Jacques Ferrier Architecture/SCP d'architecture Cusy Maraval
- Greater Paris Express scheme (project no. 15): Jacques Ferrier Architecture and Sensual City Studio
- Passenger terminal, Sète (project no. 13): Jacques Ferrier Architecture/SCP d'architecture Cusy Maraval

Photo credits

- Cover, 14–28, 42, 46, 47, 80–96, 225–8, 234, 235, 252 (middle) © Hugo Deniau
- 32 (middle row, left), 38 (bottom), 40, 65–78, 219–23, 229–33, 237–43 © Jacques Ferrier Architecture
- 30 (top row), 32 (top row, middle and right), 34 (middle row, centre), 34 (bottom row, left), 34 (top), 113–15 © Jean-Marie Monthiers
- 30 (bottom row, left) © Hervé Abbadie
- 30 (bottom row, right) © Gaston Bergeret
- 32 (top row, left), 32 (bottom row) © Georges Fessy
- 32 (middle row, right) © Christophe Demonfaucon
- 34 (middle row, left and right) © Erick Saillet
- 34 (bottom row, right), 116–21, 123–43, 147, 150–78, 182–94, 196–218, 249 (right), 250, 251 (left and middle), 252 (left) © Luc Boegly
- 36 (top row) © Stéphane Chalmeau
- 36 (bottom row) © Mathieu Ducros
- 38 (top) © Mir
- 44 © HZCAD Shanghai
- 48–64 © Pauline Marchetti and Jacques Ferrier
- 101–12 © Philippe Ruault, 122, 149, 249 (left and middle) © Philippe Ruault
- 145, 146 © André Morin
- 179, 181 from Shanghai Dreams, Laurence Thiriat, presented by Les Bons Clients in collaboration with Arte
- 195 © Jonathan Leijonhufvud
- 244–5 © Villages Nature, all rights reserved
- 246, 252 (right) © Villages Nature/photo Chantiers Modernes Construction

First published in the United Kingdom in 2016
by Thames & Hudson Ltd, 181A High Holborn, London WC1V 7QX

The Architecture of Jacques Ferrier © 2016 Jacques Ferrier Architecture
Introduction © 2016 Alexander Tzonis
Essay and interview © 2016 Kenneth Powell

Designed by Olivier Lebrun

All Rights Reserved. No part of this publication may be reproduced or transmitted in any form or by any means, electronic or mechanical, including photocopy, recording or any other information storage and retrieval system, without prior permission in writing from the publisher.

British Library Cataloguing-in-Publication Data
A catalogue record for this book is available from the British Library

ISBN 978-0-500-34312-8

Printed and bound in Latvia by Livonia Print

To find out about all our publications, please visit www.thamesandhudson.com.
There you can subscribe to our e-newsletter, browse or download our current catalogue, and buy any titles that are in print.

720.
92
FER